MW01278372

SALLY'S MOVIE DIARY

A Companion to the Novel
MISSING IN TIME

Yo Lily

Catherine Harriott

love
catherine
x x x

Copyright © Catherine Harriott
Published by Library Stamp
This Edition 2022
First Edition 2014
All rights reserved
ISBN: 1976163463
ISBN-13: 978-1976163463

ACKNOWLEDGMENTS

Big thanks to first-class beta reader
Tarissa Graves: www.Inthebookcase.blogspot.com

Images by
www.123rf.com

DIARY DATES

For Adrian

"If a person could live forever, if a person was immortal, how would they change over time?"

Danny Rubin, Screenwriter, *Groundhog Day*

FEBRUARY 2ND
Groundhog Day

Hey! Just looked at the date and it's Groundhog Day!!! Which is really, really weird because it all started with *Groundhog Day* (the movie that is, not the day).

There was no warning. No your-life-is-going-to-change-forever feeling. It was my first day of my first ever vacation at my aunt's house in England, and I was all set to watch *Groundhog Day* on her old DVD player. But I never did get to see it that night. Instead, I went back in time and accidentally took the movie with me.

If any sensible person gets a hold of this diary, they'll think I'm crazy. I have to admit it sounds crazy, but then if they knew anything about my life, they'd know I'm telling the truth.

Anyway, that's the reason I've started this. I need somewhere to write my thoughts down because they get all jumbled up inside my head, and I think I'm going to explode if I don't.

On top of that, I'm writing this diary to you, Adrian, because I want to tell you about my movies. Even though you said to me moving pictures (you always said moving pictures because you're a boy from the past) are your thing, I want to think they could have been our thing too.

And—here's what messes with my head—you may have been born 100 years ago but you're still fifteen. Which, when you think about it, is a whole three years older than me, so really you should have watched so many more movies by now. But, of course, you haven't.

Anyhow, seeing as it's February 2nd . . .

Today's Movie: **GROUNDHOG DAY**
Groundhog Day is set in a small Pennsylvanian town called Punxsutawney.

Now, every February 2nd there's a cute custom here where they hold up a furry groundhog in the town square, and if it sees its shadow then the winter's going to last another six weeks (which means a lot to the folks with cold weather in the North).

In this movie, Phil (played by actor/funny guy Bill Murray), is a TV weatherman who's bored of his job, especially as he has to cover the groundhog story every year. This year, though, he has a new female producer with him, Rita (Andie MacDowell, looking romantic with long curls), as well as his cameraman friend, Larry (Chris Elliott).

When a winter storm blows in, they all get snowbound, and the next morning we see Phil wake up in Punxsutawney to find it's Groundhog Day—again. He has to live it all over. And then day after day he keeps waking up on Groundhog Day.

This is where it could have got boring, but it never does. It's hilarious and thought provoking at the same time. Phil, whose character is selfish and sarcastic, has to get the day right before he can move on. And he can't just pretend either, or exploit people for his own gain.

Whatever the deeper meaning, I find myself watching *Groundhog Day* over and over again.

A bit like Phil.

"I was born at the age of 12 on an MGM lot."

Judy Garland, Actress, *The Wizard of Oz*

FEBRUARY 3RD
The Wizard of Oz

Well, forgot to check if the groundhog saw his shadow or not, so I don't know whether it's going to be six more weeks of winter. Though this doesn't mean much to me living here in sunny Florida.

Sunny or not, I usually find February a bit of a blah month. It's not summer. It's not spring. Even Christmas is a distant memory.

I shouldn't complain, though—it's awards season. I've already watched the Golden Globes, and the Academy Awards are just around the corner.

When I was with you, Adrian, there was no TV. Not even electricity. You never can tell what life's going to throw at you. Or when you're going to get stuck somewhere and can't get home.

My life back in time reminds me of a movie about another girl who couldn't get home. One minute she's in Kansas trying to find shelter from a tornado, the next she's dropped into a magical place known as the Land of Oz.

Today's Movie: **THE WIZARD OF OZ**
I couldn't believe it when I discovered *The Wizard of Oz* was made in 1939. The detail, the color, the special effects are all spectacular for a movie made when they didn't even have green screens.

This movie, I must tell you, Adrian, is a musical. With musicals the songs have to seem like a natural part of the plot. If not, then the whole production can seem comical, and not in a good way either. Anyway, this MGM musical is more than good, and the songs all work.

Here's the plot . . .

Dorothy (the late, great Judy Garland) lives with her Aunt and Uncle in the middle of nowhere on a tumbledown Kansas farm. To keep her company, she has a scruffy little dog, Toto. This feisty dog keeps getting into trouble, and an interfering witch-like woman is threatening to take him away and have him destroyed. Dorothy wishes she could escape. She dreams about finding a place where there's no trouble.

A place over the rainbow.

Up until this part, the movie is in brown and white—a film color known as sepia. But when a tornado uproots Dorothy's house, dropping her and her little dog in the land of Oz, she opens the door into brilliant Technicolor. This effect is a master-stroke by someone at MGM Studios, and I never get sick of seeing it. Maybe it was the idea of one of the fourteen or more writers this movie had, or maybe one of the five directors!

Back to the movie . . .

Dorothy and Toto journey to the Emerald City where Dorothy must ask a magnificent wizard there how to get home. Along the way, she meets three friends: the Scarecrow, the Cowardly Lion, and the Tin Man.

In the meantime, The Wicked Witch of the West is out to stop her. But another witch, The Good Witch Glinda, is there to help, and gives Dorothy the sparkliest ever ruby-red magical slippers. And she'll need them too, if she wants to get out of danger and return home.

MOVIE MAGIC

In *The Wizard of Oz,* actor Frank Morgan wore a vintage shabby gentleman's coat for his role as Professor Marvel (he also plays the Wizard). This coat had been bought at a second-hand store in Hollywood by MGM studio's Wardrobe Department.

One day on the set, the actor examined the coat closely, and to his surprise discovered stitched into one of its pockets the name "L. Frank Baum"—the author of all the Oz books.

In a bit of handy detective work the studio contacted the tailor who had made the coat, as well as the author's widow, and sure enough, the coat had actually belonged to Baum.

When the movie wrapped, the studio presented the coat to Mrs. Baum. And for years afterwards, because this incident sounded suspiciously like a publicity stunt, no one would believe it.

But it was true!

"You'll never find a rainbow if you're looking down."

Charlie Chaplin, Actor/Director/Producer

MARCH 8ᵀᴴ
The Kid

Movies have been around for over 100 years—a long time. Though probably Mr. Rodriguez, my teacher, would say that's not so long. Just a blink of an eye. But that's not how he'd say it. He'd probably say something clever like the blink of a Neanderthal man's eye.

Movies made in your time have no color or sound. When you were little, Adrian, people were so amazed at this new moving-picture technology they would scream, thinking speeding trains and galloping horses were coming out of the screen towards them.

You'd think there wouldn't be any more movies made in my time that were silent and in black-and-white, but you'd be wrong. *The Artist* is a movie that came from stage left to win five Oscars, and it's silent and funny and clever. Even the little dog in it can act.

On the subject of the black-and-white days, remember when I told you I'd run away to Hollywood and wait for Charlie Chaplin to arrive? Wouldn't it have been great to meet him, and other silent stars like Mary Pickford and Lillian Gish with their long, flowing locks? Or Clara Bow with her big expressive eyes.

But Charlie Chaplin was an actor who could play funny or sad. He didn't need words. The story was all in his face. He became famous for a character he created called the Little Tramp. Even when sound was invented, he still made silent classics like *City Lights* (1931), a sad, romantic movie about a blind flower girl who the Little Tramp tries to help.

Today's movie, though, is called *The Kid*. Charlie Chaplin created it from his own experiences as a workhouse child in Victorian London. It was his first full-length film, which he not only starred in but also wrote and produced!

Today's Movie: **THE KID**

The Kid (1921) is about a baby boy abandoned in the street by his mother and found by a tramp (although the tramp's not homeless). The tramp (Charlie Chaplin) raises the boy (played brilliantly by Jackie Coogan), and though they both live in real poverty they form a strong, unbreakable bond.

After five years, the pair are more like father and son, and there are some funny moments when they work in the window repair business, with the boy going around breaking windows to get business for his dad. But when the boy becomes sick, a mean doctor calls in Social Services, and they come to take him away. The scenes where father and son are torn apart are heartbreaking.

All this time, though, the mother, regretting what she's done, has been searching for her child. Will she find him, and what happens to the tramp and the boy if she does?

The poverty in *The Kid* looks very real. They don't just streak people's faces with dirt and throw around a few old props. Maybe it's the lack of color, but the poor places in this movie—garbage-strewn streets, peeling paint on bare rooms, years of finger-prints on the tramp's door—all look authentic.

In the end, though, it's the acting that counts—
Charlie Chaplin gives a great performance. But the
best thing about this movie is . . .

The kid.

Jackie Coogan as The Kid

MOVIE MAGIC

Jackie Coogan, who became mega famous playing the cute loveable boy in *The Kid,* was one of the first ever child stars of Hollywood.

You'd think that this was a good thing, but all through his childhood his mother and step-father took advantage of his success, and when Jackie grew up he found they'd spent all his millions of dollars of movie earnings. He sued. But the courts only awarded him peanuts compared to what he'd really made. The good news: the public's shock at what had happened led to the first legal protection for child actors, making studios set aside a trust fund for them.

And Jackie?

He grew out of his cute child-star status, but if you watch reruns of the classic TV show The Addams Family, you'll spot him.

He's Uncle Fester!

"I wanted her [Giselle in *Enchanted*] to be a strong character with her own light shining from inside."

Amy Adams, Actress
Enchanted
Catch Me If You Can
Big Eyes

MARCH 18TH
Enchanted

Today, I'm dreaming about the future and wondering did I ever tell you, Adrian, I so bad want to be an actress?

But is this just a fairytale?

I mean, would I even be good enough? I want my career to last, to be different, but I don't want people to know my name, but say, "Look, that's 'what's-her-name?' She was in that thing. You know the one? The one with 'what-chama-call-it?' Anyway, she should be in more things."

But how do I go about achieving my dream? Do I have to move from Florida?

Of course I have to move. No one ever made it staying in the Sunshine State.

But should I go to acting school or try to get discovered doing extra work? I know you have to have a photo first. How do I even go about getting a headshot? When the time comes, I think I'll have a black-and-white one taken—much more flattering and retro. One day, I hope a casting director will see it and say, "Let's have her in our movie."

In the meantime, if someone could just wave their magic wand.

Today's Movie: **ENCHANTED**

Enchanted has everything a classical Disney fairytale should have: A magical land, furry singing animals, an evil queen, a handsome prince, and an innocent girl who looks and sings like a princess.

But here's the twist.

The innocent girl, Giselle (the lovely Amy Adams), is thrown from her animated world into another dimension—modern-day, hard-hitting, dream-crushing New York.

In this real world she meets Robert (Patrick Dempsey). He may have princely good looks, but he doesn't believe in true love. He is a divorce lawyer, after all. His daughter, Morgan (Rachel Covey), does believe though, and she adores the wide-eyed and innocent Giselle, who turns their world upside down.

Woven into this magical movie are dozens of shout-outs to Disney classics, such as *Snow White and the Seven Dwarfs, Cinderella,* and *Sleeping Beauty*. There are hidden Disney references too: A bus driver's hair is shaped like Mickey Mouse ears; Robert works for the law firm Churchill, Harline and Smith, which are the names of the songwriters from *Snow White and the Seven Dwarfs*. And, although not from a Disney movie, Giselle even makes clothes out of the drapes the way Maria does in *The Sound of Music*.

Adrian, you need to seriously catch up on all these classic movies, but I think you'll find *Enchanted* has the best blend of life-action and animation there is, and Amy Adams as Giselle makes it all seem believable.

"You say, 'Oh, I'll do that [movie], that's amazing. What a great story'. . . and then your job is to try and make the audiences feel like you felt when you first read that script, that feeling you got—wow—the journey."

Danny Boyle, Director/Producer

Millions

28 Days Later

Slumdog Millionaire

127 Hours

APRIL 3RD
Millions

Oooh, so little time, so many movies to watch.
Millions of them. And if I'm serious about acting—
and I am, whatever Gran says—then I've got to see
EVERY movie ever made.

Which reminds me, *Millions* is a great movie. I
first watched it without ever seeing the trailer. I
loved watching the whole 98 minutes, clueless about
what was going to happen next. Exciting (and I don't
use the word lightly) just not knowing anything. And
that gets me thinking about movie trailers.

MOVIE-TRAILER VOICE . . .

In a world where Sally has to be at the Cine-plex early for the best seat (left-hand corner, top row) and not miss one single piece of dia-logue from up-coming blockbusters, she is devastated to discover she does not—horror—want to see any more movie trailers. Does not want to hear the best lines, see the best special effects, or know what the ending is!

Seriously, it's a love/hate relationship with trailers. On the one hand, I want to experience the whole movie as it unfolds on the screen. I want to be wowed. On the other hand, trailers are great appetizers and fun. So I'll probably still sneak a peek now and again.

Today's Movie: **MILLIONS**

Millions is a movie about two young brothers coping with the death of their mother, and how they deal with a sudden windfall of a large stash of cash.

Anthony (Lewis McGibbon) is the older brother, and much to his embarrassment his younger brother Damian (Alex Etel) talks to dead saints—yes dead saints—which we get to see on screen, shivering halos and all.

When the boys and their trying-to-keep-it-together Dad (James Nesbitt) move into a new house, young Damian drags a bunch of leftover packing boxes to a field to create his own fort, and seemingly out of nowhere drops a bag of money from the sky.

Now his brother, Anthony, is something of a wheeler-dealer and he tries to advise Damian of the best way to spend this windfall. Basically, Damian looks for ways to give the money away to good causes, and Anthony looks for ways to have mega fun with it.

There are lots of laugh-out-loud lines, and I like the way the brothers look out for each other. Both boys give natural performances; maybe because they weren't experienced actors at the time.

And the director, Danny Boyle (of *Slumdog Millionaire* fame), is one of the best. Someone once said if you could get the American way of making a movie LOOK GOOD and combine it with the British way of making a movie SOUND GOOD, then you'd have the perfect movie. Danny Boyle does that, and I hope one day he'll put me in one of his.

"It would actually be really interesting if Spider-Man died. Why doesn't the superhero ever die? I think if Mary Jane was alone . . . she could give birth to a spider baby and carry on the series with another young boy or something like that."

Kirsten Dunst, Actress

Spider-man

Jumanji

APRIL 9TH
Spider-man

Pop quiz Adrian: If I'm avoiding trailers, how do I choose a movie to watch, you may ask.

Well, sometimes I pick a movie because of the director, or it has a particular actor I admire in it. Sometimes, I like the sound of the storyline, or there's a buzz about it that sparks my interest. Other times, I read the tagline and get a nice I'd-enjoy-it feeling.

Occasionally, a movie turns out to be better than its description, and even though, for instance, it may be an action adventure, it also has characters you care about, and a perfect beginning, middle and end.

I mean, a boy bitten by a spider, who turns into a spider-man, and then leaps from building to building while a green goblin is chasing him, doesn't sound that promising. Does it?

But it is.

Because *Spider-man* has proper character development and plenty of quiet moments in-between the action. So you care.

Today's Movie: **SPIDER-MAN**

Peter Parker has a friend called Harry who is tormented by his dad's disappointment in him and tries not to be envious when his dad makes it obvious that he admires Peter more.

Then there's the girl they both want: Mary Jane.

Peter lives next door to Mary Jane (Kirsten Dunst) who is sad and vulnerable and doesn't notice him much until one day when they talk and she finds he's really supportive and kind.

"You're taller than you look," she tells him.

Later on, little does she guess the secret he has to hide – his spidey superpowers.

At first, Peter enjoys these powers. But as he learns, "With great power comes great responsibility," he realizes he must change into a serious fighter for good over evil. Including fighting Harry's dad.

But will all the sacrifices he has to make, be too hard to handle?

The main role in this movie, Peter Parker, who turns into Spider-man, is played by the quiet actor Tobey Maguire. He has an everyboy quality about him. You can see him as the Peter Parker part: shy, small, not that noticeable. So it's all the more impressive he makes it work when he turns into the muscly Marvel hero.

The special effects are amazing too, and look great in 3D or not. Either way works.

"This film [*Somewhere in Time*] moves me
more than you can know."

Christopher Reeve, Actor

Somewhere in Time

Superman

APRIL 11ᵀᴴ
Somewhere In Time

Adrian, some movies stay with you forever. They may not be on anyone else's top ten list, but they are special to you. Because a special movie is usually one that somehow connects with your life — even if it's about an alien from another planet, or is set in another time. Sometimes, you just recall the cinematography or the music or the mood. At some point, as you're watching this movie, you may get goosebumps or the shivers. And after you've watched it once, it stays with you. Usually for days, but parts of it you'll remember forever. Like . . .

Today's Movie: **<u>SOMEWHERE IN TIME</u>**

You may guess from the title that this movie is about time travel. But *Somewhere in Time* is really a love story. Even though it's a science-fiction movie, there isn't much science behind the time travel, but that doesn't matter. The main theme throughout is about love at first sight. I don't cry often over a movie but there's something about the longing, the loss, and the music that stirs my emotions.

Here's the outline . . .

Richard (the late, great Christopher Reeve) sees a vintage photograph of a woman called Elise (Jane Seymour), and he feels connected to her somehow. He can't stop thinking about her, or wondering what her expression may mean. Can you fall in love with a person in a photograph? Well he does. And he's got to go back in time to find her. He's staying at a Victorian seaside hotel, and he discovers that the woman he's fascinated with once worked there as an actress.

Can he find her? And if he does, will he stay with her forever?

Will all the obstacles in his way, including time itself, ever be overcome?

EXTRA: *Somewhere in Time* has a cult following, and there's even a group of fans who meet every year on Mackinac Island, the movie's location, where horse-drawn vehicles are still the main mode of transport. But at the time this movie came out, people were expecting the main actor, Christopher Reeve, to be in another action role, as he was just coming off the back of his *Superman* fame. It took a while for it to find its true audience, and because of my own journey back to the past and meeting you, Adrian, I'm definitely one of them.

MOVIE MAGIC

Jane Seymour, who plays Elise in *Somewhere in Time,* first got noticed in Hollywood when she auditioned for the role of a glamorous Bond girl, and not just because of her unusual eyes (she has one green eye and one brown) or her acting skills. This is how she stood out from hundreds of other actresses trying for the part.

Jane was waiting to chat to a James Bond producer about the Bond-girl role. She was sitting among actresses who were all dolled-up and in full make-up. But Jane had a scrubbed make-up-free face, and her hip-length auburn hair was hidden under a hat. She knew she had to do something dramatic to stand out.

So, when it was her turn to audition, halfway through sitting in front of the producer, she casually pulled off her hat, and her long, long hair tumbled over her shoulders and nearly touched the floor.

She was hired on the spot!

Jane Seymour in Somewhere in Time

"As a youngster, I never dreamed there could be a career actually earning a living writing music."

John Williams, Composer

Jaws

Jurassic Park

Harry Potter (first three movies)

Close Encounters of the Third Kind

Raiders of the Lost Ark

Star Wars

APRIL 12ᵀᴴ
Jurassic Park

Sometimes, I think wouldn't it be great if your life had its very own soundtrack. Perhaps some upbeat music playing when you're striding down a city street. Or soothing music when you're stressed. How about some mellow music if you're kind of sad. Or dramatic music when you're feeling extra emotional.

An amazing score or soundtrack can make a movie memorable. I mean, imagine *Jaws* without its something-terrible-is-about-to-happen hum.

Or *Jurassic Park* without its big sound to go with its big dinosaurs . . .

Today's Movie: **JURASSIC PARK**

Pop quiz: Can dinosaurs ever be brought back from the past to live in our time? That's the question this movie asks.

Dr. Alan Grant (Sam Neill), a Paleontologist (a person who digs up and studies old bones and fossils), is a serious character who, much to his assistant/girl-friend's (Laura Dern) dismay, is not interested in having children—ever.

Turns out though, the way he treats kids Tim (Joseph Mazzello) and Lex (Ariana Richards) like adults, works well in this Steven Spielberg directed blockbuster about a theme park with real dinosaurs and the mayhem they cause when they get loose.

The scientist, John Hammond (Richard Attenborough), behind the theme-park idea—think Islands of Adventure but with real monsters—can't be persuaded that his dream is dangerous until it's too late. Mainly because a resentful and hard-up computer geek employee decides to steal some valuable live dinosaur eggs, after first shutting down the security system that keep the dinosaurs locked behind high-voltage wires, enabling the dinosaurs to escape.

Trapped in the park, can Dr. Grant, Tim and Lex escape the deadly dinosaurs and save the day?

Jurassic Park is a great adventure movie, and at the time it was made the special effects pushed all the boundaries. The dinosaurs today still look awesome and lifelike as they stomp around with that dramatic soundtrack in the background.

And who knows, one day we may find a way to bring them back.

"I am insecure. If you ask me, everybody is."

Kate Winslet, Actress

Titanic

Sense and Sensibility

Eternal Sunshine of the Spotless Mind

APRIL 15TH
Titanic

I woke today with a black-cloud feeling that I just can't shake. Why aren't you here, Adrian? When I'm with you, I feel ready to take on the world. But when you're gone, my confidence just melts away. Today, especially, because I'm going to have trouble watching *Titanic*. You would too.

Or maybe you wouldn't?

Maybe you'd think the story about Rose and Jack, two young people from two different worlds—one rich, one poor—had nothing to do with what we went through.

What we suffered has made me realize that when something has happened to people from the past, you can read a book or see a movie about it, but you can't live it. It's not real. It can't hurt you. You're protected by the pages of the book or the movie screen. But when you're there, hemmed in by the crowd, touching coat sleeves, hearing voices as you try to breathe because it's happening. Then you know how it really was.

The way it happened to us.

Today's Movie: **TITANIC**

It's 1996, and Brock Lovett (Bill Paxton) and his adventurous maritime team are at sea, searching for the wreck of the *Titanic*. They're also searching for a valuable diamond called the Heart of the Ocean, thought to have been lost with the doomed ship.

When news of the *Titanic* discovery is screened on TV, Rose, a lovely 101-year-old woman (Gloria Stuart), recognizes herself in a portrait the explorers have found. After calling Brock Lovett on the phone, she is flown to the ship, and tells him her story in a wonderful flashback to 1912.

SPOILERS AHEAD: Rose is now seventeen (played by Kate Winslet), and she arrives with her family at Southampton docks, ready to board the *Titanic*. Looking gorgeous in Edwardian clothes, she steps from a horse and carriage, and we meet her fiancée, who we sense through their conversation is not her true love.

On board in the first-class staterooms, we witness Rose's relationship with her controlling mother as she tugs her into a tight-laced 1912 corset. The mother is forcing Rose into this marriage, mainly for financial reasons. Rose later realizes, as she watches a little girl being taught 1912 dinner-table manners, that she's been groomed all her life to obey. She can't breathe and has to run and run. She wants her life to end.

Jack (Leonardo DiCaprio), a young and charming poor artist from third class, comes to Rose's rescue, and their relationship begins. But her mother and fiancée disapprove and try to split them up.

At every opportunity Rose and Jack try to escape to be together—and many scenes that follow show us the life of the third-class passengers below compared to the life of the privileged first-class ones up top (sound familiar, Adrian?).

When the ship hits an iceberg and is in danger of sinking, Jack sets out to save Rose, and we are taken minute-by-minute through the events of that fateful night.

And when we flash forward to modern times, we find out whether Brock Lovett ever discovers the priceless Heart of the Ocean diamond.

Adrian: The most moving part of the movie for me is the scene just before the end credits. I won't give it away, but I like to think that's how everything ended in real life.

Or you may want to watch another *Titanic* movie called *A Night to Remember*. I don't know whether it's the moody black-and-white cinematography or the lack of special effects, but it transports me back to that time even more.

MOVIE MAGIC

The character in *Titanic* who reminds me most of the people I met in 1912, is old Rose (played by Gloria Stuart) because of the way she moves and speaks, taking her time, and the way she's so dignified. Gloria was in her eighties when she played Rose and had to have ageing make-up to make her look over one hundred!

In real life, Gloria was born in California in 1910 on a dining table. She had a varied and interesting career as a beautiful actress and artist, and died exactly a hundred years after her birth. But she was the only person in the movie who was alive at the time of the actual sinking of the *Titanic*.

"When I was really young, I didn't know that there was such a thing as a screenwriter. I wrote stories."

John Sayles, Screenwriter
The Secret of Roan Inish
The Spiderwick Chronicles

APRIL 16TH
The Secret of Roan Inish

To take my mind off yesterday's *Titanic* mood, I'm cleaning and organizing my room. I just can't help it. I've even rescued some old ice-cream tubs and stuck labels on them. Now I can put all my old movies into neat categories.

Example . . .

A is for Action and Adventure.

I never used to be this way. My room was like a warzone. But ever since I was a servant back in your time, I've been unable to be untidy. Gran says I must have got over my messy phase—the one that lasted all my life.

On the subject of organizing, I've just found my

big purple notebook with sparkly silver stars on the front. That's where you'll find my alphabetized tabs with personal pages for each actor I like, and a list of MUST-SEE movies. I've enough to keep me going for about two years.

So I think I'll take a break and watch something, because cleaning makes me think of Fiona and Eamon from *The Secret of Roan Inish*. They cleaned and repaired a bunch of cottages on a deserted island; even patched up their roofs. I've never seen anyone enjoy fixing up a house as much as those two.

Today's Movie: **THE SECRET OF ROAN INISH**
Fiona (Jeni Courtney) is a girl from the city who goes to live with her grandparents in a teeny-tiny seaside village. She learns from them that she's descended from a selkie. This is a seal that turns into a human being on the land.

Weird.

On top of that the seals have stolen her baby brother, and Fiona keeps spotting him running along the cliffs. (The baby creeps me out a bit. I think they dyed his hair.)

Anyway, Fiona wants to get her brother back,

and with her cousin Eamon's help, sets about the task. The two of them also try to bring back to life the abandoned island where her grandparents once lived.

Throughout this movie, Jeni Courtney as Fiona is a natural. When she walks barefoot, I imagine I'm walking barefoot. When she stirs a pot of tar, I feel as if I'm stirring the pot.

The Secret of Roan Inish brings back memories of us living by the sea, and, set in Ireland, this movie is worth watching for the cinematography alone. I find it peaceful, and when I've had a busy day, I like to get lost in its lyrical magic.

"I love women who have fought to change the world and made a difference."

Drew Barrymore, Actress/Producer

E.T. the Extra-terrestrial

Ever After

The Wedding Singer

Never Been Kissed

Fifty First Dates

APRIL 20TH
The Ghost and Mrs Muir

Yay! It's Saturday, and Gran just rewarded me with a PJ Day for cleaning my room.

It's not her fault, but she can't afford to give me an allowance or send me to the theme parks. Instead, I get these days where I can stay in cozy-comfy PJs all day long. It's funny, but I really seem to need more PJ Days since I came back from your time period.

Anyway, here are the rules, invented by me . . .

PJ DAY RULES *(good ones)*

Rule #1

A PJ Day is 24 hours long. Half a PJ Day does not count—it has to be the full day until the next morning.

Rule #2

PJ Days cannot be interrupted for outside chores, not even to haul out the trash to the sidewalk or check the mailbox at the end of the drive.

Rule #3

A sick day is not considered a PJ Day.

Rule #4

If a PJ Day has to be interrupted for any reason, and I have to get dressed and go out, then a full credit PJ Day must be given.

Possible reasons for interrupting a PJ Day:

a) We have to evacuate to an emergency shelter because a category five hurricane is on the way.

b) There's no chocolate left in the house, and I have to do a store run (OK, Gran might not give me a credit PJ Day for this emergency).

c) The end of the world is coming (on second thoughts, I think I'll stay in my PJs).

So now I've explained the rules, I'm going to enjoy my PJ Day watching an old comfort movie from the black-and-white days.

I'm drawn to this movie for so many reasons. I feel I know the main character, the age she lives in, the seaside village she moves to. I know it's an old movie but that doesn't matter. The more I watch movies, the more I'm drawn to old classics.

This one, set at the beginning of the 1900s, is a story about a woman's dream of finding independence during a time when women were not supposed to be independent. Adrian, she reminds me so much of Lydia who wanted to become a suffragette back in your time.

Today's Movie: **THE GHOST AND MRS MUIR**
Lucy (Gene Tierney) is a young, beautiful widow living with her jealous and interfering sister-in-law and her emotional mother-in-law.

One day, Lucy decides to escape to the seaside with her young daughter Anna (Natalie Wood) and her faithful female servant Martha (Edna Best). However, her sister-in-law tries to persuade her to stay put—probably because she wants to keep bossing her around.

SPOILERS AHEAD: At the seaside, Lucy's realtor also tries to boss her by keeping her from viewing a house he thinks is unsuitable. Lucy stands firm, and despite the fact it's haunted by a sea captain (Rex Harrison), Lucy takes the house.

Then the fun begins.

The sea captain ghost tries to scare her away, but Lucy has had enough of being bossed and decides to stay. The captain is impressed, and they connect through long conversations together and even writing a book. Later on, a man in the real world wants to win her love. But all is not what it seems.

The Ghost and Mrs. Muir won an Oscar for cinematography, so I spent a whole screening just studying the camera work and the way shadows and light are used. I think people and places look beautiful in black and white, don't you? I also love the stirring music by the great composer Bernard Herrmann, so I'm putting the soundtrack on my wish list.

EXTRA: It's haunting when little Anna says in *The Ghost and Mrs. Muir* that she loves the sea, because in real life the actress who plays her, Natalie Wood, actually drowned at sea.

Rex Harrison and Gene Tierney in
The Ghost and Mrs. Muir

"A lot of my life happened in great, wonderful bursts of good fortune, and then I would race to be worthy of it."

Julie Andrews, Actress/Singer

The Sound of Music

Mary Poppins

MAY 10TH
The Sound of Music

The best, best part of a movie for me is usually the opening. I love the way stories are set up, and I get all settled in with a bag of popcorn and bar of chocolate, and I close the drapes and turn the lights down. I have this big fluffy cushion. It looks like a purple movie prop from *Legally Blonde,* but it's the squashiest thing I own, and I wouldn't give it up for anything because it wraps around my shoulders at just the right spot and it took at least twenty movies to get it that way.

Today's Movie: **<u>THE SOUND OF MUSIC</u>**

This musical has an uplifting opening that makes your heart soar. It's best viewed on the big screen where you'll feel like you're on top of a mountain.

Here's the plot . . .

Maria (Julie Andrews) is a nun in an abbey in Austria. But she's not a particularly good nun, and the other nuns don't know what to do with her. The Mother Abbess (Peggy Wood) decides to send her away to work as a governess to the seven children of Captain von Trapp (Christopher Plummer). Maria is devastated to be leaving the abbey, but the Mother Abbess tells her in a song not to be afraid, to hold her head up high.

When Maria arrives at the wonderful and elegant mansion that's to be her new home, she learns the wealthy and distinguished naval Captain has forgotten how to show his children any affection. In fact, he's seriously strict, even calling them with a whistle as if they're all under his command.

Also, since his wife's death, there's no music in his life. Maria brings back the music, teaching his children how to sing and play and—well—be children again. She even makes them some play clothes out of the drapes.

The eldest girl in the von Trapp family is sixteen-year-old Liesl (Charmian Carr). She has a crush on Rolfe (Daniel Truhitte), a boy who delivers telegrams. But there's danger ahead. It's the beginning of World War II, Hitler has marched into Austria, and Rolfe has joined the Hitler Youth. When the Captain refuses to report for war duty, Rolfe is torn between his loyalty to the Nazi party and his fondness for Liesl and her family who he's known all his life.

Meanwhile, the Captain is engaged to a Baroness, who plans to pack the children off to boarding school.

Will Maria return to the abbey and abandon the family? Will Captain von Trapp be forced to join the Nazis? Or will he escape and marry the Baroness? Or does fate have something completely different in mind?

Adrian, the songs from *The Sound of Music* were all created by the talented song-writing duo Rodgers and Hammerstein, and Julie Andrews singing them as Maria is the best. Julie was also a star of the stage and that is how she got discovered for her role as Mary Poppins, which I'll tell you about tomorrow.

"Sometimes opportunities float right past your nose. Work hard, apply yourself, and be ready. When an opportunity comes you can grab it."

Julie Andrews, Actress/Singer

Mary Poppins

The Sound of Music

MAY 11TH
Mary Poppins

I just made lunch, and Gran wants to know why I keep making these tidgy sandwiches with the crusts cut off. That's the trouble with time traveling, you pick up some weird habits.

Actually, it's funny watching her woof them back in one mouthful. She wouldn't survive in the stuffy Edwardian times with its oh-so-correct manners, which is the period today's movie is set in. Adrian, this is my second Julie Andrews movie this week, but I think you'll relate to it because this one is set in England in your time.

When I was with you there, I never met anyone like Mary Poppins or her friend Bert. Nobody said, "Spit-spot." Nobody said, "Say no more, Gov'ner." I don't know what I expected. We were in Yorkshire most of the time, and Yorkshire folk have their own special way of saying things.

Anyroad—as you would say—one thing's certain, when I was a servant, I didn't expect anyone to click their fingers to clean a room. Now that would have been handy. I really could have done with Mary Poppins' cleaning skills.

Today's Movie: **MARY POPPINS**

Mary Poppins (Julie Andrews) is a magical nanny who comes umbrella floating down from the sky to the Banks' family home in Cherry Tree Lane, London, where children Jane (Karen Dotrice) and Michael (Matthew Garber) live.

Now, the children's father, Mr. Banks, is a man who likes everything prim and proper and under his control. He's annoyed because Jane and Michael keep driving away their nannies. But when Mary Poppins turns up for the job, she flips roles and takes charge by interviewing him—love that.

Mary is a no-nonsense but loving type that soon

whips the whole household into shape, and Jane and Michael have exciting magical times, especially when they meet her friend Bert (Dick Van Dyke).

But running through this story is the way Mr. Banks has trouble showing affection to his wife, who's a suffragette but still obeys him, and to Jane and Michael—he's missing out on their childhood, Bert tells him through a song.

What makes this movie a classic is Julie Andrews as Mary Poppins. She just bursts off the screen with stage presence. And like any good magical nanny (such as, Nanny McPhee), she leaves when she's supposed to. When she's not needed anymore.

"One person's craziness is another person's reality."

Tim Burton, Director/Producer

Edward Scissorhands

Charlie and the Chocolate Factory

Beetlejuice

Alice in Wonderland

The Nightmare Before Christmas

MAY 16TH
Edward Scissorhands

When I time travel, my hair grows as normal, but when I come back on the date I left, I have to trim it so people don't think me strange. Which reminds me of a character called Edward Scissorhands.

He likes to cut hair.

Today's Movie: **EDWARD SCISSORHANDS**
Edward Scissorhands is a movie about a man-made boy created by an inventor who was unable to finish him, so the boy's hands are made of scissors. And although the boy sometimes moves with Pinocchio like stops and starts, we believe he is real because

of his haunting eyes and the emotions he feels.

One day, after the inventor has died, the boy Edward is rescued from his lonely life by the Avon lady, Peg, a soft-spoken, soft-hearted mother. Peg takes him home to live with her family, where he falls for her quirky daughter.

When Edward ventures outside into the family's 1950s cookie-cutter-style neighborhood, he's a huge hit, especially with the bored stay-at-home wives who let him cut their hair; until a series of misunderstandings cause them all to turn on him.

One of the themes of this movie is how fame affects people. But all Edward wants is love and understanding and to fit in. He tries so hard, but the harder he tries the more things go wrong.

And the director, Tim Burton (*Beetlejuice*), really captures this movie's mood: The bright sunny colors of the neighborhood's look-alike houses contrast well with the dark house on the hill where Edward Scissorhands lived alone in the shadows.

In fact, everything about this movie feels perfectly made. The sets, the music, the script: It all fits together without flaw.

"If you took acting away from me, I'd stop breathing."

Ingrid Bergman, Actress

Casablanca

Spellbound

Joan of Arc

JUNE 1ST
Casablanca

Remember when I was back in your time, Adrian, I used to tell you about movies from my time? All those standout lines and catchphrases. It was funny because you didn't have a clue what I was talking about.

I bet screenwriters never know what lines are going to become famous when the movie they're working on is released. Lines like "You're gonna need a bigger boat" from *Jaws*. Or "There's no place like home" from *The Wizard of Oz*.

Sometimes, it's not the line so much but the way it's delivered. Like the way Rupert Grint as Ron in the first Harry Potter movie says about Hermione, when she thinks that being expelled from Hogwarts is worse than being killed: "She needs to sort out her priorities!" It's not that funny, but the way he says it always gets a laugh.

Sometimes, though, a line gets remembered in a movie that was never said: "Play it again, Sam" is often quoted as being from *Casablanca*. But people mix up two actual lines from the movie said at different times by different people: "Play it once, Sam" and "Play it."

But there are so many memorable one-liners in *Casablanca* that I can't keep track. Lines like:

"Here's looking at you, kid."

"We'll always have Paris." And . . .

"I think this is the beginning of a beautiful friendship."

Today's Movie: **CASABLANCA**

It's 1940s Casablanca, a city in Morocco under French rule, and this is where we find Rick (Humphrey Bogart) at the beginning of World War II, running a bar and trying to keep his nose out of Nazi business.

Rick's so cool about everything, it looks like he's got it all figured out, but when he sees lost love Ilsa

(Ingrid Bergman) sitting in his bar, we know he's been hiding a secret past.

Ilsa is a soft-spoken natural beauty with an amazing European accent. Easy to understand why anyone would fall in love with her. But all through this movie a question hangs in the air: Why did Ilsa once leave Rick stranded at a train station with his heart shattered into a thousand tiny pieces?

Actually, there are a couple of other questions in this movie: Will Rick stand up against the Nazis? And will he take Ilsa away from her freedom-fighting husband?

The role of Rick is played by one of the most famous actors of all time, Humphrey Bogart, who usually plays tough guys. That's why it's interesting to watch him here, playing a character who is trying to keep his emotions in check in a love story that doesn't feel like the usual.

In *Casablanca,* Humphrey Bogart has lots of memorable lines, and the camera loves Ingrid Bergman's face, which always looks like it's being lit by its very own star. In the end, though, it's this couple's chemistry together that shines—the pain, the passion, the longing—it's all there.

MOVIE MAGIC

In the early days of movies, actors were larger than life. They came from the world of stage theater where they had to exaggerate their movements to project to people sitting in the back row. The close-up had yet to be invented.

By the 1930s and 40s, actors like Humphrey Bogart, James Cagney, Burt Lancaster, Catherine Hepburn and Bette Davies filled the screen with their presence.

As Bette once said:

"Acting should be bigger than life. Scripts should be bigger than life. It should ALL be bigger than life."

Bette Davies

"I was whoever they wanted me to be."

Natalie Wood, Actress

West Side Story

Rebel Without a Cause

JUNE 5ᵀᴴ
West Side Story

Humphrey Bogart and Ingrid Bergman in *Casablanca* makes me realize on-screen chemistry is one of those rare things. It's not forced, it just is. Which is how all the best screen couples are.

COUPLES THAT CLICK . . .

- Robert Redford and Barbra Streisand in *The Way We Were*. Was it all so perfect in the past for these two? Or like the song says, has time rewritten every line?

- Billy Crystal and Meg Ryan in *When Harry Met Sally*. Timing is everything in this relationship.

- Bogie and Bacall (Humphrey Bogart and Lauren Bacall) especially in *To Have and Have Not*. This couple actually ended up getting married in real life when this movie wrapped.

- Gregory Peck and Audrey Hepburn in *Roman Holiday*. They're so right together, you can't bear to see them part. I mean, there's something about a relationship being forbidden that makes it more emotional.

Today's Movie: **WEST SIDE STORY**

West Side Story is a finger-clicking, toe-tapping version of Romeo and Juliet: Shakespeare's original story about forbidden love. And the couple who play them have real chemistry.

Here's the outline . . .

Maria (Natalie Wood) and Tony (Richard Beymer) are associated with two rival New York gangs, one Caucasian and one Puerto Rican: The Jets and the Sharks. The only safe place members of these two gangs can meet without fighting is at the local gym where supervised dances are held. It's at one of these dances that Maria and Tony fall in love, and because their love is forbidden, they have to plan to meet in secret.

Meanwhile, the gang fighting is spiraling out of control. Will Tony, who is trying to pull away from his gang, be able to avoid all the trouble so he can find a place to live his life with Maria in peace? Or will the street violence pull them into a place of no return?

West Side Story is so good it won best this, best that, best everything Oscars. Ten wins altogether, which is unusual for a musical.

EXTRA: Elvis Presley was originally picked to star in *West Side Story* but his manager turned it down for him. When the movie came out it was said Elvis regretted his manager's decision.

"This really should be kept secret, but you can learn a lot by watching the making-of [movies]. Every actor should do it. You figure out what you're dealing with."

Bill Murray, Actor

Groundhog Day

Ghostbusters

JULY 11ᵀᴴ
Back to the Future

It's late, and I'm in bed flicking through the channels with my remote control.

Well, watching a movie on TV is all fine and good, but it's great to buy movies because then you get the special features like background interviews, making-of movie clips, and funny out-takes. I love these extras because when you're enjoying a movie, you don't want it to end.

It's like your very own backstage pass.

Today's Movie: **BACK TO THE FUTURE**

Back to the Future is part one of a science-fiction trilogy featuring Marty McFly, a teenager who goes to the past (not the future) in a DeLorean car that's been converted into a time machine by an Einstein-type scientist called Doc Brown (Christopher Lloyd). The title comes from the fact Marty must return to the future from the past.

Adrian, you and I know messing with time is a dangerous thing. Time can play tricks back. And the more you try to fix things, the more you have to chase the consequences. And Marty definitely flaps some space-time continuum wings, changing the events of his life for good. In the meantime, he has to deal with a bully, his parents' first date, and his mother's obsession with—him!

Marty is played by Michael J. Fox. Because the studio wanted him so much for this role, they asked him to shoot the film at night after he had spent all day on his daytime TV acting job in the classic sitcom Family Ties.

Phew!

In *Back to the Future* something about Michael's must-be-on-caffeine energy and the way he enthusiastically says his lines, makes you believe each piece of the plot. And each line or camera shot has a purpose, and you find yourself going back to watch this movie (and its special features) again and again.

"I am very, very clear on how difficult it is for a young kid out there to go into the arts without taking a lot of heat from his peers."

Patrick Swayze, Actor/Dancer

Ghost

Dirty Dancing

JULY 21st
Ghost

When Demi Moore was filming the movie *Ghost*, the director asked her if she could shed a tear during a scene. "Yes," she said, "which eye do you want?"

Bruce Almighty!

I'm having trouble trying to cry from both eyes. Perhaps I should just practice raising one eyebrow. That looks really good on screen, that whole arching one eyebrow thing.

Talking about Demi Moore, I love her gravelly voice. Which makes me hope I have an interesting voice for my movie career. I don't mean breathless like Marilyn Monroe, but full of character like Holly Hunter. Because if you have a standout voice, you often get offered parts in animated movies or voiceovers, which is a big bonus.

John Hurt (he played Mr. Ollivander in the Harry Potter movies) has an interesting voice that's been used for tons of voice work.

Another Harry Potter actor, Alan Rickman, who played Snape ("Clearly, fame isn't everything, is it, Mr. Potter?") has a deep voice that sounds scary. But Morgan Freeman (*Bruce Almighty*) has a deep voice that sounds wise.

A unique kind of voice is Christopher Walken's (he played the dad in *Catch Me If You Can*). It's not his tone that stands out but more the way he constructs his sentences, pausing in unusual places.

Back to Demi Moore . . .

Today's Movie: **GHOST**

Despite its name, *Ghost* isn't a scary movie. It's a love story about Sam (Patrick Swayze) who in life finds it hard to share his feelings with Molly (Demi Moore):

Molly: I love you.
Sam: Ditto.

It's also a movie told from the viewpoint of the ghost. How he has to deal with still being on earth. And how he has to find a way to protect Molly from danger when she doesn't even believe in the spirit world.

The cast, from Demi Moore (who shocked the director when she turned up on day one of the shoot with short hair, though it really suits) to Oscar-winning Woopie Goldberg as a reluctant psychic, are outstanding, including: Tony Goldwyn as best friend Carl; Rick Aviles as the bad guy running scared; and Vincent Schiavelli as a subway ghost in a bad mood.

Patrick Swayze is also just right for the lead part, though other actors passed on this role because they didn't think being a ghost would showcase their talents.

How wrong were they?

The screenwriter, Bruce Joel Rubin, won an Oscar for *Ghost*. And like all well-written scripts, every scene and line has a purpose to move the story along. I also like the different ways he finds for Sam to communicate to the living, like lifting pennies in the air, or magically writing on a mirror or computer screen. There's a tender, satisfying ending, too, but I won't give it away.

"I think you can learn [screenwriting] by watching movies, and I think you can learn by doing, but I don't think somebody can tell you. You either have your intuition or you don't."

Caroline Thompson, Screenwriter

The Secret Garden

Edward Scissorhands

Black Beauty

AUGUST 4TH
The Secret Garden

Right now, I'm homesick for Robin Hood's Bay. Which is strange because that's not my real home.

Our life there was so intense, wasn't it, Adrian? But I really miss the winding stepped streets of our little Yorkshire seaside village. And watching the next movie, *The Secret Garden*, reminds me of the gardens at Brumpton Manor where we lived. There's a gate in the wall there, too. Though ours didn't have a key.

Today's Movie: **THE SECRET GARDEN**

I keep noticing that tons of movies were books first. Books are so rich in detail and story that it must be hard for screenwriters to figure out what to keep in and what to leave out.

The Secret Garden (1993 version) was a classic book first, written by British/American writer Frances Hodgson Burnett. Caroline Thompson wrote the screenplay. She also wrote screenplays for *Edward Scissorhands, Black Beauty,* and *City of Ember,* so she's really talented.

Here's the story . . .

Mary Lennox (Kate Maberly), a pale and sulky orphan girl, has to leave the warm climate of India and go live at her uncle's home at Misselthwaite Manor in frost-covered Yorkshire, where she finds it hard to adjust. (Sound familiar, Adrian? A girl from a warm climate lands in Yorkshire and finds it hard to adjust?)

Well, this homesick girl, Mary, is warned by the Manor's horrible housekeeper (Maggie Smith of Professor McGonagall fame) to keep out of trouble and not to go wandering about. But when Mary hears strange wailing sounds in the dead of night, she just has to go investigate.

In a giant four-poster bed, she finds a small, sickly boy, Colin (Heydon Prowse) who thinks at first, she's a ghost. But the boy is so pale she thinks he's a ghost too.

Mary and Colin (who are really cousins)—along with Dickon (Andrew Knott) a soft-spoken local boy who has a special bond with animals and nature—are drawn together and bring back to life a secret garden behind a locked wooden door. But that's not the only thing brought back to life, which is sort of the theme throughout.

The music and cinematography for *The Secret Garden* really draws you into the mood of this corner of Yorkshire. The garden holds secrets and magic, and the three main characters all help each other in different ways.

Adrian, I think you'd really relate to the local boy, Dickon. Not so much Colin who is spoiled, though he's so funny and tragic with it. Mary is unloved and also acts spoiled, but I admire her strong personality and the way she takes charge.

Anyway, I'm enjoying yearning for my York-shire home, so I'm going to watch *The Secret Garden* again, and maybe even read the book.

"After auditioning hundreds of kids, I threw the DVD [David Copperfield] on her [casting director's] desk. 'This is the kid I want! Just bring him to me!'"

Christopher Columbus, Director (talking about finding Daniel Radcliffe for the role of Harry Potter)

AUGUST 5ᵀᴴ
Harry Potter and the
Prisoner of Azkaban

The Secret Garden movie made me realize sometimes settings are so vivid they become a character in their own right. Hogwarts School is like that, for instance, especially in the third Harry Potter movie: *Harry Potter and the Prisoner of Azkaban*. The one directed by the talented Mexican film director, screenwriter and producer Alfonso Cuarón—who also directed *A Little Princess* and *Gravity*.

He definitely has that magical touch.

Today's Movie: **HARRY POTTER AND THE PRISONER OF AZKABAN**

All the Harry Potter movies have something special to offer but the first movie and the third are, for me, the best.

The first movie because I'd just finished reading the book at the time, and I felt I was actually walking into the pages as the film unfolded onscreen. Gran says everyone was so quiet when the credits rolled, you could have heard a wand drop.

The third movie because the director really achieves the magic a Harry Potter movie should have. *Harry Potter and the Prisoner of Azkaban* is full of atmosphere and wide-angle shots—silver clouds rising above Hogwarts, the driving rainstorm during Quidditch, and Christmassy snow scenes at both Hogwarts and Hogsmeade.

Also, I like the third one because out of all the Harry Potter movies, the director brings the best out of Hermione's (Emma Watson's) character, and it shows.

Plus—a big plus—I now love this movie because Hermione takes Harry (Daniel Radcliffe) back in time.

Harry: "You mean we've gone back in time?"

Hermione: "Yes. Dumbledore obviously wanted us to return to this moment. Clearly, something happened he wants us to change."

They do have something to change, but the main danger in the movie is that a murder convict from Azkaban prison has escaped and everyone thinks he's after Harry. Floating ghost-like prison guards known as Dementors are sent to search Hogwarts. They are so scary; they can suck the soul right out of a person if they want. One messes with Harry, and I love the cure Professor Lupin (David Thewlis) gives him: chocolate. Now that's my type of cure.

Without giving too much more away, the plot weaves in and out of the past and the present, and the three friends—Harry, Ron and Hermione— must, as in all the Potter movies, save the day. But this time, they get help from unexpected quarters: a real live werewolf and a growling black dog. Though not in the form you may think.

MOVIE MAGIC

At the start of the shoot of *Harry Potter and the Prisoner of Azkaban,* the director Alfonso Cuarón, who was new to the Potter world, wanted to know if his lead actors understood their characters. So he assigned Harry (Daniel Radcliffe), Hermione (Emma Watson) and Ron (Rupert Grint) a written essay, asking them to describe their characters feelings and thoughts.

After a couple of nail-biting days, Daniel Radcliffe handed the director one page of writing.

Emma Watson gave him sixteen pages (probably all numbered with lots of headings and footnotes).

But Rupert Grint didn't even turn his in.

The director was first annoyed at Rupert, wanting to know if he was taking his role seriously. Rupert told him he was being true to his character.

Ron would never hand his homework in!

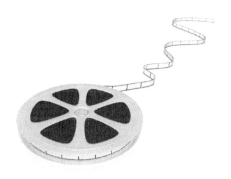

"Always believe in yourself. Do this and no matter where you are, you will have nothing to fear."

Hayao Miyazaky, Animation Director/Producer
Studio Ghibli

AUGUST 11ᵀᴴ
Kiki's Delivery Service
Spirited Away
Howl's Moving Castle

Disney is famous for animation, so is Pixar, and both studios usually use computer-generated images to help create their wonderful movies.

But one of the best at hand-drawn animation artwork is Studio Ghibli from Japan. You just have to watch *Kiki's Delivery Service* to hope that two-dimensional artwork will always live on.

Another fact about Studio Ghibli is they usually

make the lead character a girl—awesome. Other movie studios often decide the hero should be a boy. It's all about box-office revenue. They say boys won't go see a movie about a girl. But I think boys will watch a movie about a girl. They may not brag about it to their friends—wouldn't be cool— but they do.

So, Adrian, what we really need is more girl power in Hollywood to give us more girl leading roles. But not in weak girly, girl movies. It should be real stories about real girls having real adventures. Just like Studio Ghibli's movies . . .

Today's Movie(s): As these are my top three Japanese Studio Ghibli movies, I'm going to tell you about their American versions together.

KIKI'S DELIVERY SERVICE

Kiki is a young witch who, upon reaching the age of thirteen, must fly away from home to learn her craft. She arrives (or crash lands) in a seaside town, where she discovers new friends, especially a boy called Tombo; and in order to survive, finds a job delivering baked goods on her broom.

Number one about *Kiki's Delivery Service* is the artwork. Every little cobblestone, leaf and raindrop is painstakingly drawn. When Kiki flies on her broomstick over the seaside town, the detail draws you in, and you want her to land there and make it her home.

Number two is Kiki (Kirsten Dunst) herself. She is fun, feisty and adventurous, and I wish I had her people skills.

Number three is, I love the world Kiki lives in, but when she's homesick, I can totally relate. To help her she has, of course, her new friend Tombo, but also a motherly baker, and this funny cat called Jiji, who reminds me, Adrian, of our black cat Smudge.

Kiki's Delivery Service was the first Studio Ghibli movie I saw and, although there's no big action plot, it's one I watch over and over.

SPIRITED AWAY

The heroine in this movie is not a witch but an ordinary girl, Chihiro (Daveigh Chase), who has to deal with moving with her family from the city to the suburbs.

On the way there, they take a wrong turn and arrive at what looks like a closed-down theme park. When her parents are spirited away to another world, Chihiro must discover how to free them. And with the advice of a helpful boy called Haku (Jason Marsden), she must handle monsters and spirits and find out who she can trust.

So much imagination has gone into this movie. There are ghostly characters, fat blobby ones, one is dragon-like, and others are cute balls of sooty fluff. I also like that the director (Hayao Miyazaki) is not afraid to have quiet moments that last longer than those usually shot in animation.

Spirited Away won Best Animated Oscar, and I'm glad because it was so different from anything I'd ever seen.

That is until I watched the next movie . . .

HOWL'S MOVING CASTLE

Howl (Christian Bale) is a gorgeous wizard who lives in a magical castle. A castle that not only can stand up and walk through the countryside but can also land in different places in time and space at the turn of a dial.

Sophie (Emily Mortimer) is a sad eighteen-year-old girl, who spends her days working in a hat shop making hats, though her own hat is plain and simple to go with her plain and simple clothes.

When a spoiled and nasty witch (Lauren Bacall) casts a spell on Sophie, she turns her into a 90-year-old woman (voiced by Jean Simmons). Horrified, Sophie runs away, finds Howl's castle and makes it her home.

Adrian, I watched this movie twice in one sitting, not only to enjoy the artwork but so I could fully understand the plot. It gets a bit complicated trying to work out all the different characters and the roles they play in a war that Howl doesn't want to fight in.

But I can relate to Sophie because she has to clean house to survive, the way I did in your time. And the characters in the castle: the young apprentice wizard Markl (Josh Hutcherson) and Calcifer (Billy Crystal) a fire demon with a sense of humor, all become like family.

In the end, though, this story is about love and loss and war and doing the right thing.

The music is moving, too.

"I don't want to dress up a picture with just my face."

Grace Kelly, Actress/Princess

Rear Window

To Catch a Thief

Dial M for Murder

AUGUST 27TH
Rear Window

Phew! It's middle-of-the-summer hot, and Gran can't afford the air conditioning again. My hair's stuck to my face, and I've had to wipe down the mold off the pages of my movie book "One Hundred Years of Classic Movies."

I've just finished the Hitchcock chapter. I've seen nearly all his films (I'm writing 'films' and not 'movies' because he's a British director), including *Rear Window*, *Vertigo*, *The Birds* and *Psycho* (don't tell Gran about this last one 'cos it's a bit of a horror).

Adrian, I thought about Hitchcock movies a lot back in your time. Whenever I peered down at the cottages from my attic room, I thought of the man that spies on the homes in *Rear Window*. Whenever seagulls woke me, I thought of *The Birds*. And when I felt dizzy time traveling, I thought of the same feeling the character has in *Vertigo*. I tried, though, not to think of the movie *Psycho*. Just the chilling music alone makes me hide under the covers and sleep with the lights on.

Anyway, to make me feel I'm not the only person without air conditioning, I'm going to watch *Rear Window*. Gran should be happy, there's no blood, no gore, not much gun action, just edge-of-your seat excitement. And you totally get drawn into the lives of the people.

Today's Movie: **REAR WINDOW**

Rear Window opens with a snapshot into the life of daring photo-journalist L. B. Jeff Jefferies, or Jeff for short (James Stewart). He's wheelchair bound day and night in his sweltering New York apartment, recovering from a broken leg. Bored, he starts noticing the lives of the people who live in the block of apartments opposite.

His glamorous model girlfriend, Lisa (Grace Kelly, who in real life goes on to become a royal princess), his police friend, and his down-to-earth nurse, all think he's gone stir-crazy with the heat when he's convinced one of his neighbors has murdered his wife and hidden the body.

Lisa, though, is smart and eventually decides Jeff needs her feminine intuition to solve the case. We learn she'd like to be his wife. But Jeff doesn't think she can handle being hitched to a man who travels the world with only one small suitcase. She sets out to persuade him he's wrong, including putting herself in danger.

Everything in this movie—the wide-open windows of the apartments opposite, the neighbors who sleep outside on their balconies, the sweat running down Jeff's face—reminds us this is New York before air conditioning.

A bit like my room.

"Being an actor is the loneliest thing in the world . . . you're all alone with your concentration and your imagination and that's all you have."

James Dean, Actor

Rebel Without a Cause

Giant

East of Eden

SEPTEMBER 18TH
Rebel Without a Cause

Meet James Dean. He only acted in three movies but they were all classics. He died young, living on the edge, so he'll always be remembered as this good-looking guy who invented cool. He still looks cool.

He was one of the first Method actors—that's where actors use their own emotions and memories to help them give a realistic performance. Instead of acting they actually *feel* what their character is going through, whether that's pain, guilt, sorrow, joy, or any other emotion.

James also got some of his acting inspiration from watching animals' actions. See him in *Rebel Without a Cause* where he curls up in a ball like a cat and pounces. It's a bit like Hugh Jackman when he channels wolfs as Wolverine.

Of the three movies he made, you feel sorry for his unloved character Cal in *East of Eden*. You cheer for his character Jett in *Giant* when he hits it rich. But the coolest character he plays is Jim in . . .

Today's Movie: **REBEL WITHOUT A CAUSE**
Jim Stark (James Dean) is a teenager with problems I can relate to when he says: "If I had one day when I didn't have to be all confused and I didn't have to feel that I was ashamed of everything. If I felt that I belonged someplace. You know?"

On top of that his mom and dad are driving him crazy: "You [Mom] say one thing, [Dad] says another, and everybody changes back again!"

The only thing good in his life is his new girlfriend, Judy (Natalie Wood). But she's got parent issues, too. Especially a father who refuses to show her any affection.

And Jim's parents have just moved him to yet another town, yet another school, and he must try to fit in without getting into any more trouble. But the local kids have other plans, and Jim is pulled reluctantly into their world of fights and street racing, goaded on by Judy.

Later, we meet Plato (Sal Mineo), an odd boy, who tags along with Jim and Judy, trying to get them to take care of him because his parents are never around. When Jim, Judy and Plato run from a street gang and break into an empty house in the middle of the night, they all end up in real danger.

Rebel Without a Cause tries to explain why kids from 'good' homes get into trouble. And how, if they don't have affection or guidance, they'll go out and bond with gangs for good or bad.

And James Dean? He plays his character Jim sometimes with sensitivity, sometimes with drama, and you just can't take your eyes off him. Jim is trying to be good. He's really trying. And James Dean makes you feel Jim's emotional pain, his disappointment at his father, who is weak and won't give him the man-to-man advice he craves. You feel Jim's hunger for that advice and his disgust when his father can't or won't help. You see him struggle inside between needing his parents' love and his anger at them for loving him too much, till he can't

107

think, he can't breathe, and has to somehow grow up all by himself.

James Dean

"I read [Anne's] Diary on the plane . . . and it just kind of hit me in my heart and my soul."

Millie Perkins, Actress, *Diary of Anne Frank*

SEPTEMBER 19TH
Diary of Anne Frank

Lying in bed, all I can wonder is how am I ever going to be an actor when I don't know the first thing on how to go about it. I mean, what does a girl do to jump-start her career on celluloid?

I even asked Gran if she knew. But Gran just seems to live in her own world from the past. Though she did mumble there won't be any money for drama school. When she saw my face, she suggested I go ask the school's careers counselor.

I don't know how old she thinks I am. "I'm in middle school," I told her. "We don't have one."

"Well go ask that nice teacher Mr. Rodriguez," she said.

Which is not a bad idea. At least Mr. Rodriguez is young, so he may understand and not tell me to give up on my dreams and think seriously about my academic future.

So tomorrow I'm going to pluck up the courage and ask him. I'll wait until there's no one hanging around. Difficult because Mr. Rodriguez is popular, which is surprising since he also teaches us history. I think because, apart from the list of dates he makes us remember, he always finds a way to make it interesting, like reading us true stories about real people.

Today's Movie: **DIARY OF ANNE FRANK**

One of the reasons I like this movie is because it's narrated by a girl, Anne (Millie Perkins), reading her diary. You find out her thoughts and feelings and dreams for the future.

When I lived in the past, I thought my attic room was cramped, but Anne's living in a small secret annex above a warehouse in Nazi occupied Amsterdam with—get this—her mom and dad and sister; a boy called Peter and his mom and dad; and a forty-three-year-old man who she must share her room with! Not just for a month or two either, but for two whole years, and she's not allowed to speak above a whisper until nightfall and is never, never allowed to go out. It's way too dangerous out there. Any day, their hidden-behind-a-bookcase doorway could be discovered and booted down by the secret police, and then they'll all be hauled off to concentration camps.

Just because they happen to be Jewish.

But Anne has her imagination to escape to. And her diary to get her thoughts out of her head. And Peter (Richard Beymer of *West Side Story* fame) who she grows more and more close to. To talk to and let off steam.

The whole time, though, I don't think she could have survived that long without the extra space up in the roof with its tiny window. There she could gaze at the sky and get some air and be alone or be with Peter, away from the grown-ups who argue and don't understand her at all.

Yes, Anne's words are moving, but what really gets to me is—her story is all true.

"The Havisham mansion [in *Great Expectations*] was a real house, not a studio set, although it was redressed so the great room was filled with spiders' webs that would get in my hair."

Jean Simmons, Actress

Great Expectations

Spartacus

Hamlet

Howl's Moving Castle

SEPTEMBER 20ᵀᴴ
Great Expectations

Turns out Mr. Rodriguez is also there to help with career choices and not just history lessons and nervous breakdowns.

I'm not joking. A girl in my class, Lyn Louise, had a breakdown last term. She's in an after-school music group—violin—and her parents really put the pressure on her. They kept going on about a place at New York's Juilliard.

Well, faster than you can say, "I smashed my violin into a thousand pieces," she had to leave school for a long rest.

I hope she's in a better hospital than I was back in your time Adrian.

Anyway, I've made an appointment to see him on Monday—Mr. Rodriguez, that is. Fingers crossed. Though, I'm not expecting too much.

Today's Movie: **GREAT EXPECTATIONS**

Great Expectations is a famous Dickens' story about a poor boy who, because of promises made, expects to one day come into a fortune. There are many versions of this movie, but the one I think has the most atmosphere is the classic one from the black-and-white days that is directed by David Lean.

Here's the plot . . .

Orphan Pip (Tony Wager) lives in a humble house on lonely marshlands with his mean grown-up sister (Freda Jackson) and simple but kindly brother-in-law Joe (Bernard Miles). Joe is a blacksmith, who, as you know, is a worker who hammers and shapes hard metal objects into things like horseshoes.

In the opening, we see Pip running over the marsh-lands, past a hangman's noose. The wind howls and the tree branches creek as he goes to place flowers on his parents' grave. Pip's bleak world is then turned upside down when he stumbles across a wild-eyed chained convict Abel Magwitch (Finlay Currie), who threatens him with murder if he doesn't help. Pip, scared for his life, runs home and takes a chain-breaking tool for the convict from Joe's workshop and, riskier, a meat pie from his mean sister's larder, and these events change his life forever.

Cut to a year later, and a wealthy man-hating old lady, Miss Havisham (Martita Hunt)—a woman ditched years ago on the day of her wedding (her clocks are frozen at the wedding hour and she still wears her now faded white dress)—wants Pip to be a friend to her adopted daughter Estella (Jean Simmons), who, to him, looks like a princess. There are hints of a reward and a change to his life. Estella, though, is learning to be cruel like Miss Havisham, and practices her nastiness on poor Pip.

Time moves on, and grown-up Pip (John Mills) having turned his back on his humble beginnings, now lives a gentleman's life in London. Will he ever meet the beautiful Estella again? And will new discoveries force him to face his past?

In the end, will Pip's great expectations involve the people and a life he never bargained for?

EXTRA: In Miss Havisham's manor house in *Great Expectations,* Tony Wager, who plays the boy Pip, actually saved the life of Jean Simmons (she plays the young Estella). On this particular day, Jean has to climb so many stairs holding a candle, and the day is long and she is getting tired. She let her hand fall and her dress sets on fire! Quick thinking Tony put the flames out before they could hurt her. Funnily enough, later in the movie, the script calls for his character to do the same thing for the grown-up Estella.

"I'm from the planet show business."

Christopher Walken, Actor

Catch Me If You Can

SEPTEMBER 23ᴿᴰ
Close Encounters of the Third Kind

Mr. Rodriguez says to read up on everything I can about making wise career choices. He handed me a few pamphlets. Looks like he didn't take me seriously, after all, about wanting to act.

So I've been hiding from the world under my comforter, and I fell asleep. I dreamed of a movie studio. They were filming a scene, and I was standing behind red velvet ropes and no one would let me in. Waking up, I realize I've got to have a plan. Maybe I'll go to the library and look for a book— "Careers in Film" or something. I'm such a dummy, I should have thought of that first.

Hey, maybe there's a Dummies book for actors?

In the meantime, I'm going to get lost in a Steven Spielberg written and directed movie classic.

Today's Movie: **CLOSE ENCOUNTERS OF THE THIRD KIND**

This movie is about an everyday type of guy, Roy (Richard Dreyfuss of *Jaws* fame).

One day, he witnesses a UFO and becomes obsessed with finding aliens for reasons he cannot fully explain. Especially to his family,

Meanwhile, in another connected plotline, somewhere in the middle of nowheresville a UFO is coming after a little boy inside his house. The tension builds bit by bit as the boy's mom (Jillian Guiler) tries to secure all the places some*one* or some*thing* can enter her home. You get the feeling she's not going to succeed, no matter how bravely she tries.

Back at Roy's house, Roy keeps trying to act normal, but the more he pushes away the urge to find the spaceship he thinks he's encountered, the more he's pushed to the edge. He can't even eat his dinner without turning his mashed potato into a sculpture of the mountain he mysteriously feels drawn to. His wife (Teri Garr) thinks he's gone nuts when he starts building this mountain in their living room, and Richard Dreyfuss as Roy really eats up the part as he dumps wheelbarrows of garden soil through the window, with his kids and the neighbors looking on in shock.

Finally, Roy can resist no longer and drives off to find the mountain where he believes the aliens will be. At the same time, the mother from nowheresville, who will meet up with Roy later in the stirring final scenes, sets off too.

All the locations in the third act of *Close Encounters of the Third Kind* are big and impressive: the mountain, the spaceship landing site, the heavens. And the humans seem small by comparison, including Roy, who is wowed by everything he sees.

Adrian, I get the feeling that this story opened the door to Steven Spielberg shooting his alien classic, E.T. The next movie I want to tell you about.

EXTRA:

Different Types of Close Encounters

(based on Dr. Josef Allen Hynek's classifications)

Close Encounters of the First Kind:

Sighting of a UFO at close range.

Close Encounters of the Second Kind:

Sighting of a UFO at close range that leaves a physical trace, such as holes in the ground or burn rings.

Close Encounters of the Third Kind:

Meeting E.T.

MOVIE MAGIC

Steven Spielberg chose the actress Teri Garr for the role of the mom in *Close Encounters of the Third Kind* after first watching her in a coffee television commercial. He said if she could impress him in a 30-second commercial, then he had to have her for a whole movie!

Note to self: Never worry about taking small acting parts. You never know who's watching.

"So I still believe E.T. does live somewhere out
there among the stars, and I will always believe
it, all my life."

Steven Spielberg, Director/DreamWorks Founder

E.T. The Extra-Terrestrial

Schindler's List

Jaws

Close Encounters of the Third Kind

SEPTEMBER 24ᵀᴴ
E.T. The Extra-Terrestrial

This afternoon, I went to Florida Mall just to hang out. I sat on this white bench, and while I was thinking about you I noticed a set of initials carved onto the seat.   E T

I decided it was a sign. So here I am at midnight, writing up my diary, wishing we could watch this movie together.

Just you and me.

Today's Movie: **E.T. THE EXTRA-TERRESTRIAL**
This Steven Spielberg directed movie is about a boy
called Elliott who meets a little creature from another planet, and it's the first movie that really
affected me. I was in Grade One at the time—the
same age as Drew Barrymore is as her character
Gertie (she's Elliott's cute and funny sister)—and
Gran says I sat with my mouth open from the minute the alien showed.

Anyway, here's the plot . . .

E.T. is visiting earth, and he accidentally gets left
behind by his fellow aliens who've been frightened
away in their spaceship by government scientists
scouting the woods. When Elliott wanders outside
his house, he spots E.T. and rushes home to try and
convince his older brother and Mom (Dee Wallace,
and I love the way she says Elliott with a laugh in
the middle of it) of what he's seen. There is much
friendly teasing about goblins and such from his
brother, but Mom just thinks Elliott has seen a wild
coyote. Elliott's convinced, though, he's seen something else.

He goes outside again and tries to entice
whatever it is with a trail of Reese's Pieces
chocolates (the boy's got taste).

Amazed and in wonder at the sight of E.T. he lures the little alien into his house and, ditching school, spends the next day with him.

In a short space of time, Elliott and E.T. bond. Whatever E.T. is feeling, Elliott feels. A crisis occurs when E.T. gets sick from living on earth's atmosphere, which in turn affects Elliott's health. (Adrian, I think you'd understand both buddies: E.T. who needs to go home, and Elliott who doesn't want to lose his new friend.)

Watching *E.T. The Extra-Terrestrial* again, I notice the dialogue sounds so realistic. The screenwriter, Melissa Mathison, really knows boys and how they talk. I especially enjoyed the argument between Elliott and his classmates when they're waiting for the school bus. "Zero Charisma" is a great insult. (Hey, just noticed Elliott's name starts with an E and ends with a T.)

When I first saw this movie, I was too young to understand it then, but *E.T.* introduced me to the greatness that is Steven Spielberg, and I've been a devoted fan of this director ever since.

EXTRA: There is a Dummies book for actors. It's called "Breaking into Acting for Dummies."

"I think you see in people's eyes what they've been through. Anything in their lives shows up in their eyes."

Kirsten Dunst, Actor

Jumanji

Spider-man

Little Women

The Two Faces of January

OCTOBER 11ᵀᴴ
Jumanji

After you've seen this movie, Adrian, you'll never look at board games the same. Jumanji is the name of this game, and each throw of the dice leads to danger and a get-out-of-this-puzzle or it's the end of the game in every sense of the word.

Today's Movie: **JUMANJI**

The plot of *Jumanji* follows the lives of two boy-girl friendships from two different time periods. As the movie unfolds, we learn the backstory of each couple, starting with Alan and Sarah.

SPOILERS AHEAD: Alan (Adam Hann-Byrd) is being bullied by the town's local kids, and on top of that he has a cold, strict father who, when Alan gets into trouble, threatens to pack him off to boarding school. Sarah (Laura Bell Bundy) is the friend who feels sorry for Alan, and when they begin to play a board game they've found, Alan gets sucked into the game: literally.

Twenty-six years later . . .

Judy (Kirsten Dunst) and Peter (Bradley Pierce) are two orphans who have moved into Alan's old house. They find the board game and start to play. What they don't realize is each turn releases something wild, such as a jungle animal stampede, a bad-guy hunter, or a creeping plant that looks like the attacking plant from *The Day of the Triffids*. It also releases Alan.

Alan is now grown and must find Sarah to finish the game or they'll all be trapped—or worse. But Sarah's been trying to forget the game ever happened.

She's even had therapy, and when Alan comes calling, she thinks she's having another breakdown.

Bonnie Hunt (the mom from *Cheaper by the Dozen*) plays the grown-up Sarah, and she's really funny. Robin Williams, who usually is one-of-a-kind hilarious in his roles, plays the grown-up Alan, but in this part, he plays it with a serious, panicky quality—not surprising since his character has been stuck playing this deadly game most of his life.

There's so much more to *Jumanji*, but I don't want to give away the rest of the plot. I will tell you, though, the major theme is about being able to face your worst fears.

The question is, will they all face theirs and finish the game?

"I spent a lot of my twenties just trying to make other people happy, rather than trying to figure out if doing that made me happy."

Reese Witherspoon, Actress

Pleasantville

Legally Blonde

Walk The Line

NOVEMBER 3ᴿᴰ
Pleasantville

Good news!

Great news, actually. Gran has found me an after-school program that holds acting classes! Right now I have this amazing feeling. It's the feeling I get when I listen to Irene Cara singing Flashdance or that song from Fame. I want to spin and spin and spin.

Anyway, I start in the New Year. It's at another school on the opposite side of town, and I like the idea that no one will know me.

I can be whoever I want to be.

Today's Movie: **<u>PLEASANTVILLE</u>**

This movie is about twins David (Tobey Maguire) and Jennifer (Reese Witherspoon) who travel through a TV portal into another dimension. One without color, in the world of a 1950s black-and-white TV series, in a town called Pleasantville. And everything is pleasant. On the surface, at least. But when Jennifer digs deeper, she finds everything isn't as rosy as it seems.

In the library the books are all blank. And at school they don't learn anything in geography class beyond the town's four corners. "What's at the end of Main Street?" Jennifer wants to know.

"The end of Main Street is just the beginning again," the teacher tells her; puzzled that someone should ask the question in the first place. And like the dead-end street in *The Truman Show*, there's no way out.

David, though, is happy he's in Pleasantville. He doesn't want to change a thing in this uncomplicated world where his new parents get along and his mom is always there, cooking, cleaning and caring for them. Not until he realizes that things have got to change. And the women of the town discover they can be anything they want to be.

Reese
Witherspoon

"There are a lot of wonderful scripts my agents can't believe I pass on, but I do because I can't hear the voice. It doesn't appeal to me then. I'm really careful. Unless I hear the voice, I can't do it."

Reese Witherspoon, Actress

Pleasantville

Legally Blonde

Walk the Line

NOVEMBER 7ᵀᴴ
Legally Blonde

The thought of actually going into a room full of strangers for my acting classes has made me feel nervous all of a sudden. Meeting a new class who don't know anything about me.

I mean, I can't just go up to someone and say, "Hey, I keep getting creeped out by my trip back in time, so can you help me act in this scene with you?"

What I need is inspiration from someone who has to be brave and confident and strong.

Someone like Elle Woods in *Legally Blonde*.

Again, another Reese Witherspoon movie.

Today's Movie: **LEGALLY BLONDE**

If a movie has a color, then this movie's color is pink. It's the lead character's favorite to wear and is sprinkled throughout the sets—but that doesn't make this film weak. Elle Woods (Reese Witherspoon) is a strong character, and the story is full of girl power.

Here's the set up…

Elle is having boyfriend trouble (Warner Huntington III played by Matthew Davis) and to prove she's worthy of being part of his academic family and can be considered serious fiancé material, Elle applies to Harvard Law. She leaves behind LA where she's popular and her personality fits in.

At Harvard, she's made to feel unwelcome by her serious classmates, and Reese Witherspoon plays Elle for real: West coast girly type meets East coast academia. But Elle is no dumb blonde, and when she decides she wants to prove herself for herself and not just to impress her boyfriend, the story really takes off.

What's refreshing in this movie is how all Elle's friends are supportive while the so-called clever crowd at Harvard are not. There's none of the usual cheerleader stereotype backstabbing and competitiveness.

In the end, though, *Legally Blonde* could have been just another ditsy rom-com, but it's not. It's smart and funny with lots of stand-out performances by not only Reese but also the supporting cast.

"I've learned that success comes in a very prickly package."

Sandra Bullock, Actress

Speed

While You Were Sleeping

The Net

DECEMBER 2ᴺᴰ
While You Were Sleeping

Sandra Bullock is an actress who adds those little extra touches to scenes, like giving a small skip as she crosses the road. And I figure she knew the camera would be on her feet driving that bus in *Speed* because her socks have little frills round the edges.

By the way, Adrian, *Speed* is where I borrowed the catchphrase 'Pop quiz' to start a question. The bad guy (Dennis Hopper) uses it all the time:

"Pop quiz, hotshot. There's a bomb on a bus. Once the bus goes 50 miles an hour, the bomb is armed. If it drops below 50, it blows up. What do you do? What do you do?"

Speed made Sandra mega famous, and soon after she was in another movie called *The Net*. Gran says people were just getting the Internet back when this movie was made, and the story plays on their fears of it taking over the world, or at least having your identity stolen. The thing I like most about *The Net*, though, is they make the geek the female for a change. Plus, there are lots of scenes with shout-outs to Hitchcock movies, so that's a fun bonus.

In the meantime, seeing as it's December, and I like to get in the Christmas mood by watching tales set in the winter, I'm catching up with *While You Were Sleeping*. I feel connected to this Sandra Bullock movie because of my time back with you, Adrian. It's about a lonely young woman caught in a lie she doesn't want to get out of because it keeps her attached to something she never had before—a big warm and loving family.

Today's Movie: **WHILE YOU WERE SLEEPING**
Lucy (Sandra Bullock) lives alone in Chicago and works at a downtown train station selling tickets. Each day she notices a good-looking and charming commuter called Peter (Peter Gallagher) and she fantasizes that one day they'll be a couple. He seems like the perfect guy, anyway, even if he doesn't notice her.

But then fate takes a hand.

SPOILERS AHEAD: Peter falls onto the train tracks, and Lucy comes to his rescue. He's taken to hospital where a misunderstanding leads to Peter's family thinking she's actually his fiancée. Peter is in a coma, and Lucy doesn't have the heart to tell his family she's not going to be his wife. The longer the lie goes on, the harder it is for Lucy to fess up.

In the meantime, Peter's brother, Jack (Bill Pullman), turns up and is suspicious of Lucy. But the more time he spends with her, the more he's envious of his brother. Or would be if Peter would just come out of his coma.

Can Lucy carry on like this forever? Or will her lie be discovered by Jack and ruin her relationship with her newfound family? Or will she, in the end, find true love?

While You Were Sleeping is a rom-com that's actually romantic and funny. Sandra Bullock and Bill Pullman have loads of chemistry together. And the supporting characters all have funny lines, too, especially Elsie (Glynis Johns, who played Mrs. Banks in *Mary Poppins*), and it puts me in the mood for another good rom-com . . .

"I try to write parts for women that are as complicated and interesting as women actually are."

Nora Ephron, Writer/Director/Producer

You've Got Mail

When Harry Met Sally

DECEMBER 10TH
You've Got Mail

New York often looks gritty in movies, but not in *You've Got Mail*. The director/screenwriter, Nora Ephron, loved the Big Apple and it shows—flower-filled gardens, pumpkins on the steps of brownstone houses, Christmas snow scenes—each NY season is lovingly showcased, making the city a place you wouldn't mind living in.

This NY movie is a remake of the black-and-white *Shop Around the Corner* where two shop workers fall for each other writing letters. In *You've Got Mail* the couple connect using email.

Today's Movie: **YOU'VE GOT MAIL**

Kathleen (Meg Ryan) runs a come-on-in-and-browse-around type of independent bookstore that's been left to her by her mom. Everything in her shop world is rosy: she knows books, she's part of the neighborhood, and her staff is like family.

But then along comes Joe Fox (Tom Hanks) and his mega chain of discount bookstores—Fox Books—and when he opens one near her, bit-by-bit Kathleen's shop loses business.

Meanwhile, using anonymous cybernames, Kathleen and Joe start an online relationship, blissfully unaware they actually know each other. The thing is, will they ever have the courage to meet in real life? And what will happen to these two rivals if they do?

Because Kathleen and Joe are already in relationships. There's Joe's shallow girlfriend Patricia (Parker Posey), as well as Frank (Greg Kinnear), Kathleen's boyfriend, to consider. Frank's the type of guy who likes to listen to the purr of an old electric typewriter. In fact, he's not a fan of modern technology at all and is always trying to prove his case to Kathleen . . .

Frank: "Name me one thing—ONE—that we've gained from technology."

Kathleen: "Electricity."

Frank: "That's one."

And after cleaning a house without the help of electricity, I so get what Kathleen means.

There are other lines in this movie I like to remember, such as: "I would send you a bouquet of newly sharpened pencils," which makes me want to go out and buy school supplies, and I don't even like school. (OK, Adrian, I know you had it a lot tougher than me a hundred years ago.)

And I always feel Christmassy and sad at the same time when Kathleen is decorating her tree in the shop window and it's snowing outside. She really misses her mom and, like me, wishes her mom could be there to give her advice.

EXTRA: A few things have changed since *You've Got Mail* was made. The closing of big book chains. The e-book revolution. I'm always telling Gran you can't stop technology. She says the secret is to keep up without throwing the good stuff away. Though she can't even set the stove's clock after a power cut, I get what she means. But then if it wasn't for time-travel technology—I wouldn't be here now, writing this.

"Even when I became the typical shy adolescent,
I never minded performing. I felt there was a
kind of safety, a protection about being on stage,
about losing myself in another character."

Hayley Mills, Actress

Whistle Down the Wind

Tiger Bay

The Parent Trap

DECEMBER 16TH
Whistle Down the Wind

Today is my birthday!

Adrian, I wish we could celebrate by going to the Enzian movie theater. You'd love the gardens there; so tranquil and full of oak trees draped in Spanish moss. They'd make you forget the icy winds of Yorkshire.

I've never been through the doors, but I've seen the photos online. You can sit on comfy couches or chairs and have food brought to you at your very own table. If we were there, I would pretend we were at a private screening and all the other moviegoers were movie moguls, there just for us.

Today's Movie: **WHISTLE DOWN THE WIND**

Whistle Down the Wind is a black-and-white movie about young farm girl Kathy (Hayley Mills) and her brother and sister who find a stranger in their barn and think he's Jesus! The village children get wind of this and want to meet him. But Kathy doesn't want everyone to know: "It's a secret society from the adults," she warns them, and they must never tell.

Alan Bates, who plays the stranger in the barn, gets the part just right. He's a wanted criminal, but after he meets the children, he's so quiet and gentle, you somehow want him to escape the police.

And you feel the children are saying exactly what's going on in their heads. You just don't think they're reading lines at all, especially Kathy's little bro, Charlie (Alan Barnes). I also love the way they play outside all day, running over the fields and farms with never a grown-up in sight. Adrian, our life was like that 100 years ago. At least it was on our days off.

In *Whistle Down the Wind,* I can really relate to Kathy who has no mom. Her dad though, who is strict with his other kids, always has a soft voice just for her. And she's going to need that caring voice when everything gets emotional at the end.

MOVIE MAGIC

When Hayley Mills was a girl she had many leading roles, including playing identical twins in the original *Parent Trap*. She came from a talented family. Her father is Sir John Mills, a classic actor from the black-and-white days of film. Her sister is also an actress, and her mother wrote the book, "Whistle Down the Wind," which the movie is based on and Hayley starred in.

Hayley's first acting job, though, was in the crime movie *Tiger Bay*. How she auditioned for the role is a little unusual . . .

The director (J. Lee Thompson) had already chosen Hayley's dad to play the lead detective. But despite searching the whole of Britain, he couldn't find the right leading child. One day, when he was visiting John Mills at his house, Hayley was playing a make-believe game in the backyard. As the director watched her, he decided on the spot she was perfect for the lead part, even though the role was written for a boy. I guess sometimes the right person is right there under your nose.

"I knew I wanted to do this kind of thing in school, but to actually have somebody that would bring you into that [movie] world, that was really exciting."

Catherine O'Hara, Actress

Home Alone

Orange County

DECEMBER 23ʳᵈ
Home Alone

I always wanted a big family. This house in the middle of nowhere feels empty without lots of brothers and sisters to share it with. But I guess you always want what you can't have.

Take Kevin in *Home Alone*. He gets lots of grief from his older brother Buzz, and it seems the rest of his family are always picking on him, too. He wishes they would just disappear.

But be careful what you wish for, it could come true. For instance, you could end up in another time-period like I did, or in Kevin's case, his family accidentally leaving him home alone.

Today's Movie: **HOME ALONE**

In this John Hughes (*Ferris Bueller's Day Off*) written movie, Kevin (played brilliantly by Macaulay Culkin) and his noisy extended family are off to France for Christmas. Why they want to leave their amazing warm and rich holiday-perfect house is a mystery to me. But I'm glad they do.

Anyway, after being sent up to the attic bedroom for losing his temper, Kevin gets left behind—home alone—and we know he's going to have trouble coping. He can't even pack his own suitcase. As his snooty sister says, "Kevin, you're what the French call *les incompetents*." Which is another way of saying you suck at doing things.

Not only does Kevin have to cope looking after himself but he also has to defend his home from two burglars who are planning a robbing spree in the neighborhood. Will Kevin find a way to be safe? And will his family come back in time to celebrate the holidays?

Adrian, Gran thinks *Home Alone* is too violent in places. But I think the violent bits are cartoony. The two clueless burglars, Harry (Joe Pesci) and Marv (Daniel Stern), also remind me of Laurel and Hardy from silent comedies. I almost expect Harry to say,

"That's another fine mess you've got me into" — a famous catchphrase of Oliver Hardy's when his lovable but clueless brother gets him into hot water.

The rest of the cast of *Home Alone* are also excellent. John Candy as a Good Samaritan who tries to help Kevin's mom, is perfect. And Catherine O'Hara is outstanding in the mom role; I wish she could play the mother in all movies (she does in *Beetlejuice* and *Orange County*).

As for the dialogue, there are lots of standout lines, such as: "You can be too old for a lot of things, but you're never too old to be afraid. And: "Guys, I'm eating junk and watching rubbish! You better come out and stop me!" A line Kevin shouts to the empty house while watching forbidden TV shows and stuffing his face with the biggest bowl of ice cream ever.

Another funny line is from a gangster movie Kevin is watching: "Keep the change ya filthy animal." This clip wasn't from a real movie, but were scenes made specially for *Home Alone*. And here lies one of the secrets to this movie's success: the detail. Right from the opening, every word of dialogue foreshadows the things to come, and every camera shot tells a piece of this family's story.

"As a child, I was fascinated by the stories of Dickens acting out everything in front of the mirror as he wrote it down."

Harry Lloyd, Actor (and great, great, great grandson of Charles Dickens)

DECEMBER 24ᵀᴴ
A Christmas Carol (Scrooge)

It's Christmas Eve, and I wonder what tomorrow will bring? Gran's not much good at finding presents, so I hope it's a gift card then I can choose for myself. Sorry, Gran, but it's true.

Anyway, I'll spend tonight watching movies.

Now there's a novelty.

As well as *Home Alone,* I have a special list to get me in the holiday mood. It's hard in Orlando to feel Christmassy when it's bright and sunny and warm outside, even though we always light candles with glittery Christmas scenes carved on them.

Candles hold a special place in my heart. When we only had candlelight at night back in your time, Adrian, they kept away the dark and scariness in more ways than one.

Today's Movie: **A CHRISTMAS CAROL**

I've come to realize writing this diary—I enjoy adaptations. Whether it's from books or different versions of the same movie. For instance, there are lots of movie versions of Charles Dickens books, like Oliver Twist, Great Expectations, and A Christmas Carol (there's even a Muppet version).

But the adaptation of A Christmas Carol I like best is from the black-and-white days; the movie made in 1951 with Alastair Sim as Scrooge. My favorite line is when Scrooge looks into his scary future and asks the Spirit of Christmas ghost: "Are these the shadows of things that must be, or are they the shadows of things that might be?"

Scrooge, of course, has the miseries: He leads a mean, miserable life, and he forces his clerk, Bob Cratchit (Mervyn Johns), to lead a mean, miserable life, too.

But one haunting candlelit night, his dead business partner, Jacob Marley (Michael Hordern), reaches out from beyond the grave to try to get him to change.

It won't be easy. He's spent a lifetime learning to be Scrooge.

CHRISTMAS MOVIE MAGIC

Elf

Prancer

Home Alone

A Christmas Story

White Christmas

Frosty the Snowman

Miracle on 34th Street

The Snowman

A Charlie Brown Christmas

It's a Wonderful Life

"I thought drama was when actors cried. But drama is when the audience cries."

Frank Capra, Director

It's a Wonderful Life

Arsenic and Old Lace

Mr. Smith Goes to Washington

DECEMBER 25ᵀᴴ
It's a Wonderful Life

Christmas Day!

I'm up early, relaxing on my big cushion, munching chocolate Santas, watching . . .

Today's Movie: **IT'S A WONDERFUL LIFE**

It's a Wonderful Life, directed by Frank Capra, is an American family Christmas classic, so I can't wait to share it with you.

The movie opens with an angel in heaven, Clarence, being asked to go help a man called George Bailey (James Stewart) who's in deep trouble on earth.

It's Christmas Eve, and George is standing on a bridge in the freezing snow, thinking about throwing himself into the icy river below and ending it all. Clarence needs to earn his wings to become a proper angel and this is his mission: Go down to Earth and persuade George to change his mind.

To help Clarence understand George's backstory, the movie goes into flashback. I love a good flashback and this one is exceptional.

We find out that the bad guy in this story is Mr. Potter. He owns most of the town except for the mom-and-pop mortgage company George's family runs. Through an unfortunate series of events, Mr. Potter manages to hide a wad of cash from George, and it looks like George is going to be ruined.

When George wishes he'd never been born, Clarence the angel grants him that wish, and in the second act we see what the town and people in George's life would have been like without him.

SPOILERS AHEAD: Don't read on unless you don't mind knowing the ending.

George sees that not only has his wife's (Mary played by Donna Reed) life been ruined by her not marrying him but also the whole town is a disaster because he wasn't there to save it from the clutches of

Mr. Potter's greed. In the end, all the people who have been touched by George—and that seems to be just about everyone in the town—come together to help him.

And, oh yes, Clarence gets his wings.

Merry Christmas

Adrian: By the way, Christmas pressie—two tickets to the Enzian movie theater! I take it back; Gran *is* the best at choosing a gift.

"We don't make movies to make money, we make money to make more movies."

Walt Disney, Producer/Animator

DECEMBER 31ST
Up

It's the last day of the year, and what scares me now is after all these plans I've made, obstacles are going to get in the way.

What I'm trying to ask the Universe: Will life stop me from becoming an actor?

John Lennon of the Beatles sang *life is what happens to you while you're making other plans*. And this is one of the themes of Pixar's perfect movie, *UP*.

Today's Movie: **UP**

UP is basically a story about two people and their long life together—the ups and the downs. But it's so much more than that. It's funny and sad and uplifting.

Though, I wondered when I saw the poster for *UP:* How are they ever going to make this movie watchable when it looks like it's mainly about a grumpy old man?

Cleverly, that's how.

The old man's name is Carl (Ed Asner), and the opening minutes of *UP* gives us a flashback to his childhood and the rest of his life—meeting his soul mate, their sense of adventure, their dreams and heartaches—and by the end of it you care what happens. To a grumpy old man.

Genius.

And like all great animated movies, after a minute of watching, you forget the characters aren't—well—real. For instance, Carl's friend, Ellie (voiced by the director's daughter Elie Docter, though she had to audition for the role and is perfect) bursts onto the screen, pulling off her helmet and making her hedgehog hairstyle spring into view. She is so well drawn as the female character, I want her to have her own movie.

Together, though, they make a great couple.

But life gets in the way of Carl and Ellie's plans to one day go to their dream place, Paradise Falls.

Even when Carl is alone and he ties thousands of balloons to his house so he can fly away, we don't know whether he'll make it.

Adrian : I wonder if one day we'll make our dreams come true. That I'll stop stressing about the future. It's helped, though, writing this diary to you, sharing my movies and my thoughts.

One thing.

Gran's on board now with me becoming an actress. She says I may as well put all the hours I spend watching movies to good use. She doesn't know how to help me, but she's not going to stop me either — so job done.

Or one job done.

I've still got to get my toe in the acting door. In the meantime, I'm looking forward to my after-school drama classes in the New Year. At least then it won't be like *Groundhog Day* every day.

And who knows? You may even join me. Even though Gran says you're not here. That you're just someone in my imagination. She doesn't know — how can she?

She can't turn back the hands of time.

BOOK BONUS

ON THE FOLLOWING PAGES
YOU CAN READ
PART ONE
of

MISSING IN TIME

PART ONE

JET LAG

UNLOCKING THE PAST

It's late, but I'm wide awake in Aunt Dottie's basement, having a polite mug of tea with Gran, listening to the two of them catch up. I don't like tea, so I pretend to drink it.

Gran changes her watch to British time.

"You've traveled forward in time," Aunt Dottie says, gazing at me from under her modern red-framed glasses. In fact, except for her name, everything about Aunt Dottie is modern. From her sparkly blue sweater to her cut-off yoga pants. She hasn't let her hair go gray like Gran's either. It's a nice rich brown color.

And the house.

I don't know what the rest of it looks like, but this space-age kitchen in her basement surprises me. I mean,

I thought everyone in England had flowery patterns and antique furniture. I listen to her rattling on in her British accent. She says words like aeroplane instead of airplane.

Cute.

I don't say much. I feel like I'm still up in the air on my first flight ever, among those white cotton-candy clouds.

Aunt Dottie tops up Gran's golden mug from the teapot and turns her swivel stool to face me. "You don't look like your mum," she says, "Or your dad."

I scrape my stool back from the kitchen bench and feel my face flush. I don't want her to mention my mom or my dad. That's private. Do not enter.

Aunt Dottie stares at my hair but speaks to Gran. "Zoe's hair wasn't this gorgeous reddy-brown color." She leans forward, examining me like a bug under a microscope. "Mmm, it's got bits of gold in it too."

I turn away and push my pain down. The way I always do when either of my parents are mentioned. They're both gone now. I can't talk about it.

So I study the night sky through the window and wonder what the view looks like in the day. Nothing like Orlando, that's for sure. No highway signs: Magic Kingdom this way, Universal Studios that.

"You look tired," Aunt Dottie says to Gran, and I

turn back round. "Do you want to rest tomorrow?"

Gran smooths down her seriously mixed-up red and purple dress, then brushes a hand through her gray hair that's standing up like Doc Brown's from *Back to the Future*. I'd probably find her look hilarious if I didn't have to go out in public with her.

"What d'you think, Sal?" Gran says. "How about a PJ day tomorrow?"

"What's a PJ day?" Aunt Dottie asks.

Gran coughs her nervous cough and looks at me. "You tell her."

"It's when I'm allowed to wear pajamas and hide from the world all day."

I don't tell her it's instead of an allowance.

"Sounds wonderful," Aunt Dottie says. "But I'd have thought you'd have been at those theme parks every day with your friends."

Friends? My movies are my friends. No one at school knows either. If they think it's weird I can't afford to go to the theme parks, I'm not about to tell anyone I buy second-hand movies, mostly from the black-and-white days.

"There's nothing like theme parks round here," Aunt Dottie points out. "But we can explore the village, if you like. Maybe catch a bus tour or two."

She swivels her stool back to Gran as if she's just thought of something. "Sally's never been here before. Shall I show her my photographs?" Without waiting for an answer, she slides off her stool, moves over to a cabinet, and taking a small key she unlocks a drawer and dumps a stack of brown-tinged photographs on the kitchen bench.

I try not to sigh. What is it about older people and their photographs? Gran's the same. Always trying to tell me stories about the past. Why keep dragging it up? Better to lock the past up and throw away the key.

"Look at this one," Aunt Dottie says, waving a photo in my face. "She fought for women's rights, you know."

I barely look but pretend to sift through the stack. One of the photographs drops onto the floor, and I pick it up.

It's of a girl standing in front of an old-fashioned bicycle shop with her hair blowing about. Her face is hidden by the shadowy imprint of someone's finger. The person behind the camera has ruined it. "Why even keep such a photograph?"

Oh no. Did I say that out loud?

Gran's pale shocked stare tells me I've gone too far this time.

"You know," Gran says, her hurt voice making me

curl-up inside. "Every family photograph has a story behind it, even a ruined one."

I'm about to say I'm sorry, but Aunt Dottie quickly changes the subject.

"Now, I've sorted out a couple of bedrooms for you down here."

Down here? In the basement?

She turns back to me. "You'll see when it's light just how big this house is from the outside. But I don't want you going into any of the rooms upstairs. They're all closed-up, and some are half finished and not safe."

Her voice doesn't sound cute any more, just strict. And her eyes are cold when she shrugs at Gran. "Workmen, hey?" And Gran shrugs back, as if she's always ordering workmen around too.

"What're you doing with the house?" Gran asks.

Aunt Dottie passes us a plate of chocolate cookies.

"Nothing now," she answers. "I used to run a hotel, but what with everyone going abroad, I had to close up. The cottages in the village do well with weekenders, but no one wants to stay in a manor house like this without a lift."

I bite into a cookie, letting the rich chocolate melt in my mouth. "It'd be fun to explore," I say, more to Gran than my second aunt once removed.

"I'm asking you not to," Aunt Dottie answers in that strict voice again.

"She won't," Gran says for me.

I want to start arguing my case but Gran's mouth is set in a hard line. Mission impossible.

Though Aunt Dottie's face softens as she looks at me. "Help yourself to any films. They're in your room. Your gran told me you like Hollywood and such. I usually download mine but my service is out." She looks at Gran. "Typical, hey?"

Gran nods as if we even have downloaded movies. "Sally watches a movie before breakfast."

"My morning movie is like your coffee," I say, suddenly feeling the need to defend my life. "It wakes me up."

"Well, you're on holiday now," Aunt Dottie says, stopping our argument. "So like I said, help yourself."

"Thanks," I mumble.

I gaze round at all her shiny stainless steel appliances. We'd better not invite her back across the pond. Even our washing machine does a thumping dance on the spin cycle. Not to mention our dishwasher's kaput. But look over there—a flat-screen TV in the kitchen—awesome. "What's that?" I ask, pointing to a large opening in the wall.

"That?" Aunt Dottie says, looking over.

"That's a dumbwaiter."

"Pop quiz: What's a dumbwaiter?"

Gran doesn't look up. She's used to me saying pop quiz to start a question.

But Aunt Dottie pauses as if I've said something foreign, before saying, "It's like a little lift for sending dishes up and down between floors. Very handy when I used to run the hotel. You just pull on the rope to make it go up or down." She turns to Gran. "It's bigger than they normally are. I was going to convert it to electric but, what with closing down the hotel, it didn't seem worth it."

"Does it still work?" I ask, my hands itching to go over and pull on the rope.

"I haven't used it in years," Aunt Dottie answers. "I think the rope's twisted."

I jump off my stool, ready to walk over to the dumbwaiter.

Gran coughs again and stops me. "Bed, I think, Sal."

Jeesh! She never lets me do anything.

But as I head for the kitchen door, I console myself with the thought that I'm here all week. Plenty of time to explore later.

UPSTAIRS

Passing the forbidden stairs, I pull my suitcase on wheels into the bedroom I'll be staying in for the next wonderful, chore-free week. My five-star room, bathroom en-suite, has—get this—a whirlpool tub, complete with a row of fancy unopened shampoos, conditioners and bubbles. I'll definitely be soaking in that tomorrow.

Gran taps on my door. "Amazing house, eh?"

"You kiddin'? Not like ours."

Gran looks offended. "There's nothing wrong with our house."

Nothing wrong? Does she stay at the same address as me? Broken doorsteps, cracked walls. Tucked away in the woods all on its own without a neighbor in sight.

She hovers next to my suitcase.

"You could have been nicer to your aunt."

"You know I don't like talking about the past."

"The past can be full of stories. Same as I told your mom." Her blue eyes have a sad, far-off look.

"Oh, Gran—"

"I know, I know," she says. "You can't turn back the hands of time."

I try to think of something nice to say, but she starts bugging me about keeping the room tidy. I close my ears. I've heard all Gran's scripts before.

"Are you listening?" she asks. "I can't step on your floor at home without snapping old DVDs."

My movies may be in one big mess to Gran's picky eyes, but to me they're in organized, alphabetical stacks. Is it my fault that the stacks get kicked about a bit and spill into each other? I mean, what's her problem? I leave enough space to cross the room.

"Just remember, this isn't your home." Gran heads to the door. "Goodnight, then."

A goodnight hug is left hanging in the air between us. Tired of her lectures, I push the hug away as I push the door closed. I feel guilty immediately and open the door again, but she's gone.

Now I throw my suitcase on the bed, casting a quick glance at the corner bookcase filled with movies. I'm trying not to be mean, to be polite to my aunt and patient with Gran, and not be ashamed of our house. But I don't think Gran gets it. That this is my break from school where I always have to pretend my life is something else. Something better. Like theirs. I'm so mixed up. I just need to hide in a movie.

But I should try and sleep in this time zone.

I unzip my suitcase and rummage through it, scattering socks and underwear and my thumb-stained copy of One Hundred Years of Classic Movies. I'm up to the Hitchcock chapter: Director of Suspense.

The only thing I can find for sleeping in is this white cotton nightgown Gran bought for me with her pawn-store money. Yes, Aunt Dottie paid for our flights, but Gran had to sell a bunch of things so we won't be treated like charity cases in a foreign country. I yank out the nightgown and make a face. Gran's got to be kidding me. This shapeless thing? And check out the old-lady lace on the sleeves and hem. She must think I'm a hundred or something.

But I pull the nightgown over my head anyway, and as I glide across the room, I have to admit, it does feel nice trailing the floor. Like one of those ladies from my movies in the black-and-white days.

Aunt Dottie's movie collection—how could I resist?—

makes me feel right at home. She even has *Groundhog Day*. Now I've got my old favorite to watch if I can't sleep. I should be able to, though. It's lovely and Florida warm in here, what with the heating cranked up so high.

But when I climb into bed, I toss and turn, thinking about everything that's happened since last week. Last Saturday actually, when Gran announced that my second aunt once removed had called to say I was going to England.

At first I was excited, especially when I looked over at the *Enchanted* calendar on the wall and seen February 10th circled. Half-term break. Only one week away. That meant Big Ben, London Eye, Leicester Square movie premieres here I come. But when I'd found out we were going to Yorkshire not London, Gran had seen my dropped-shoulder reaction and reminded me that she'd never been on a plane when she was at middle school.

And another problem. Gran was coming with me.

The thing is, I've never had a mom since I was a baby, so Gran watches me like a detective. I suppose that's why Dad never let me do anything risky when he was alive. Once, four years ago last summer, before he was sick, I wanted to go on this trip with the class. We were going sailing on Lake Kissimmee, and he told me how to punch an alligator in the face in case I fell in. But he changed his mind and never let me go. It's hard to have friends if you can never do anything, and now Dad's gone and Gran has no money, so I still can't go anywhere.

OK, I decide, kicking off the heavy covers, even if I'm not in London, at least this is somewhere different. Going to England is different. And as Bill Murray says in *Groundhog Day*, anything different is good.

For a while, I think about being on my first vacation ever and how flying was so exciting and how I'm in a foreign country and I can't wait to see it all tomorrow. The time slips by, and I still can't sleep. I try to read my book but I can't focus and keep reading the same sentence over and over.

May as well watch a movie.

There's no player in here, so I climb out of the cozy nest of my bed, throw my robe on, stuff *Groundhog Day* inside my pocket and head for the kitchen. Maybe I'll find a player in there.

I do feel a bit weird though, wandering around someone's house on my own, even if I am a relation. But I can't stare at the ceiling all night.

Flicking on the kitchen's bright lights, I notice a player on a shelf under the flat screen TV.

It's not hooked up.

On my way back to my bedroom I see the stairs and ask: What's the point of being here if I can't explore this big rambling mansion? This may be an amazing basement but it's still a basement. Anyway, blame it on the jet lag. Or the fact we don't have any stairs. But next thing, I'm on the floor above, opening doors.

* * *

The first room I try, I can't tell what it once was. All the furniture is covered in dust sheets, and there's a fireplace, half demolished.

But this next room looks like a hotel dining room, what with all these round tables and chairs and that long side table, probably used for putting dishes of food on. Oh, and there's the dumbwaiter. The little elevator in the wall. I go poke my head in. It's pretty big for just plates. It could hold a person if they scrunched up tight.

I'm about to touch the rope when I hear a noise on the stairs.

Is Aunt Dottie coming? Or, worse, Gran? Gran's going to think I'm ungrateful. She'll want to keep track of me for the rest of the week. I've got to hide. I eye the room. But where? There are no curtains or dustsheets to hide behind in here. No cupboards to crouch in. The tables don't have tablecloths to crawl under. My eyes turn to the dumbwaiter. I hoist myself up and pull down the door.

Darkness closes in. It's like I'm sitting in a shaking box. I won't be able to stay more than a couple of knee-bending minutes. I try to keep steady, but my body feels too heavy, suspended here in the wall. I can't breathe. What am I thinking? I've got to get out of here. I lift the door up and strain to listen. I can hear a clock ticking. That's all. No one's coming. I'm about to move when a rumbling noise starts below my feet.

Bruce Almighty! Is the thing going to break and tumble to the ground?

WHAT'S HAPPENING?

"Help!" I call out.

I edge my way forwards. The dumbwaiter shakes and I'm pushed back. The dumbwaiter drops—I scream—and it stops as if my scream had commanded it to. Now the dumbwaiter's stuck in the chute, and I'm clinging to the sides in scary blackness.

"Help!" I call out again.

Why doesn't Gran come? My heart's pounding. My palms are sweating. I'm afraid to move a single inch. If the dumbwaiter falls again I could trap my hands on the wall. I could *lose* my fingers. I could *lose* my toes. I curl up into the smallest, tightest ball and clench my teeth.

The dumbwaiter descends.

My stomach stays at the top but the rest of me falls.

I'm in a Tower of Terror and I want this to end. But it doesn't end. What's happening? One minute I'm in my bedroom, now I'm falling in a dumbwaiter. Nightmare.

That's it! I'm having the most fantastical falling dream. It's the thought I cling onto as I reach out and try to hold on.

But now the chute isn't there anymore, and I'm not going straight. I'm spinning and spinning and sparkling lights fly past.

At last the dumbwaiter slows—rises—stops with a jolt and—feet first—I fall out.

PANIC

I wait for the world to stop spinning so I can run from Aunt Dottie's basement kitchen back to my room.

But this doesn't look like her kitchen.

Everywhere is full of dark shadows of every size and gruesome shape. I scream and grab onto the dumbwaiter. It feels harmless again—solid. I jump back in and hold on.

Nothing.

I shake the dumbwaiter, but I'm scared it might break, so I jump back down. My heart's racing; I can feel it thumping as I hunt with my eyes for the door. There are two: a closed one on my right and an open one on the far side.

But my feet won't move.

I'm sweating. But at the same time, I shiver.

Stay calm. Stay calm.

There's a dim light on the other side of the open door. It's spilling part way into the room onto hanging saucepans. Some as large as cauldrons. Where am I? A lower floor, perhaps? Dug under Aunt Dottie's basement. I stare at the open door. Above it I can see a row of bells. Why? Are they left over from her hotel? This is definitely not her kitchen. That big black stove wasn't in it. Or that rocking chair. I hold my breath.

It's empty.

My breathing starts again. This time too fast. I take a couple of cautious steps and bump into a table. Something rattles on it. Something heavy. I want to hold onto the table, but I daren't touch a thing. Footsteps. I hear footsteps. The room swims: the pans, the bells, the stove, the chair, start to fade. A buzzing noise. In my ears. Louder.

Everything goes black.

ALSO BY CATHERINE HARRIOTT
in either Ebook or Paperback

MISSING IN TIME

Sally's struggling to survive. She's fallen into another time, another place, and only a forbidden friendship with Adrian Merryweather, a young footman, is helping her cope with the harsh life of a servant she's tumbled into.

Why has this happened to her? And will she ever get back to her own time now that she knows the dangers ahead?

Or by messing with time has Sally ruined everything?

Set in the enchanting seaside village of Robin Hood's Bay, Yorkshire, England, in the strict Edwardian world of yester-day, Missing in Time is the story of two friends fighting to stay together and the true dramatic events that unfold one hundred years ago.

ORLANDO TIPS FOR BRITS

A comprehensive travel guide covering everything a British visitor needs to know to prevent holiday stress while visiting Orlando. Written in an easy-to-read style, discover tips on dining-out, driving on the roads, using the right words, theme parks, shopping and much, much more.

Printed in Great Britain
by Amazon

82475420R00119